RED SKY MORNING

Mark,

Enjoy the adventure

[signature]

Andrew J Rafkin

Outkirts Press, Inc.
Denver, Colorado

The opinions expressed in this manuscript are solely the opinions of the author and do not represent the opinions or thoughts of the publisher. The author represents and warrants that s/he either owns or has the legal right to publish all material in this book.

Red Sky Morning
All Rights Reserved.
Copyright © 2008 Andrew J. Rafkin
V3.0 R2.2

Cover Photo By Andrew J Rafkin

This book may not be reproduced, transmitted, or stored in whole or in part by any means, including graphic, electronic, or mechanical without the express written consent of the publisher except in the case of brief quotations embodied in critical articles and reviews.

Outskirts Press, Inc.
http://www.outskirtspress.com

ISBN PB: 978-1-4327-1942-5
ISBN HB: 978-1-4327-2241-8

Outskirts Press and the "OP" logo are trademarks belonging to Outskirts Press, Inc.

PRINTED IN THE UNITED STATES OF AMERICA

PRAISE FOR RED SKY MORNING

"Andrew, a gifted story teller relives the summer he turned 17 in this coming of age fast moving adventure as a member of the crew on a commercial fishing boat.
"Red Sky Morning" is a gripping seafaring adventure written for anyone who loves the ocean." —Midwest Book Review

"From the moment I opened the book *Red Sky Morning,* I was captivated. Each chapter brought forward a new adventure or trial, and my heart raced as I looked forward to what happened next.
"This is a wonderful book. You don't have to like fishing or the ocean to appreciate the great quality of this novel. I would recommend *Red Sky Morning* to anyone, young or old. It's easy to read and hard to put down." —Bryan Draper, Aced Magazine

"Red Sky Morning is a fascinating peek inside the life of a commercial angler. Andrew Rafkin has the talent for narrating a story and bringing it to life. This gripping tale is a must read for sportsmen." —Debra Gaynor, Review Your Book.com

OTHER NOVELS WRITTEN BY ANDREW J. RAFKIN

"Creating Madness has a nonstop action-filled plot. Rafkin combines technology with likable characters and a plot ripped from the headlines. Fans of Cussler and Clancy will want to add Andrew J. Rafkin to their must-read authors." —Review Your Book.com

"A strong plot, technical savvy and a comprehensive understanding of global political positioning combine to make this a cutting edge novel of international intrigue. Compelling, timely, and believable, a great read. Look forward to Mediterranean Madness, the next in the series of O.R.C.A. adventures." —Midwest Book Reviews

"Picking up nearly where Creating Madness left off, the second book by author Andrew J. Rafkin brings all the characters of his first book back, including those who pose a threat to the world's population, and adds some new, enriching and expanding the story.
"Mediterranean Madness is a multi-layered story with a plot like a five layered cake, rich and deep."
—Donna Russo Morin, author of The Courtier's secret

I'm sixty one years old, president and owner of Palos Verdes Security for over thirty years.

My wife and I live in a seventy-eight year old house on the bluff overlooking Angel's Gate lighthouse, entry to the Port of Los Angeles.

I love the ocean, and go sport fishing as much as I can. In the near future, I plan to retire, and build a fifty-eight-foot catamaran sportfisher, which has been a life-long dream.

I have a great wine cellar and carry on the family tradition of making wine like the Croatian and Italian fisherman of the past.

I wrote most of this non-fiction true-life adventure at my office. I read excerpts of the story to my manager to see if she liked it. Carri said she did, and found the story to be similar to one told by her grandfather, who was a commercial fisherman and almost lost his life in a storm. Upon further discussion, it became apparent that her grandfather, Ike Ventimiglia, was on the *Diana*, and that we had pulled him out of the net, and I resuscitated him. It truly is a small world.

Ike just passed away. He was in his eighties and lived near Redding, California. Thinking about Ike inspired me to work harder to complete *Red Sky Morning*.

Strangely, I've somehow come full circle from my past

to the present. In the early morning while having a cup of coffee, I watch boats like the *Diana* making sets for fish off of Cabrillo Point.

The San Pedro fishing fleet has dwindled down to a dozen boats or so. The fisherman of the past made a good living, but today they can barely make it. Most of the fish are gone, and in the recent years, squid—better known as calamari—have become popular. If it wasn't for the local squid fishing, I don't think the local fisherman could survive.

Forty-four years ago, when this "true-life-adventure" began I was fishing on the *Western Ace*. My dad, the captain, pointed to these huge Russian trawlers that were dragging the bottom indiscriminately, catching every living creature that would go into the net. Dad said that type of fishing method would wipe out the cod fishing industry on the East Coast. His prediction came true. Indiscriminate fishing methods like that, along with long lining and gill netting, are now being restricted or banned.

Today we face a lot of challenges. Our world has become a lot smaller. Countries throughout the world are forming alliances to address these problems and are also starting to be more aggressive about over-fishing and the polluting of our oceans.

The oceans are our life source! We have the technology to change the course we're on. It will require a worldwide effort to protect and preserve our biggest asset, our oceans.

I'm going to fulfill my dream, and build that boat. I hope that my friends and I will continue to enjoy the sport of fishing. I also hope that our families, and especially my grandsons, will have the opportunity to enjoy the ocean and fishing as much as I do.

I developed a tremendous respect for the ocean, the weather, and the men who ventured into this life. It was rough and dangerous work, and being exposed to the weather and the sun made a man appear older than his age. They chose this way of life, though, and I saw it in their eyes—a fisherman's eyes—always searching, with gleam of optimism, determination, and a few more wrinkles than normal

Chapter 1

I felt the warmth of the morning sun on my face. A new day, Saturday, perfect for a round of golf. The sunrise was exceptional. Huge thunderheads rolled across the horizon creating a fantastic backdrop, the sun's rays reflecting a panoply of color across the sky. The mid-September weather patterns typified the time of year.

Seasonal storms off the Southern Pacific coast of Mexico generated the unstable weather.

Across the border, they called the storms *chubascos,* that blew the thunderheads through the southern deserts of California and into Arizona. The locals there called it monsoon season, complaining about the humidity.

I was sitting on my patio, having a cup of coffee and enjoying the view, when my wife, Lynn, came out.

"Good morning honey. Want some breakfast?"

"Thanks, but I'm going to have breakfast at the club. So, what are you going to do today?"

"Oh, Diane and I are going shopping at the South Coast Plaza. Then we'll find a nice place to have lunch, so you better plan to eat at the club when you finish your round. When's your starting time?"

"Around nine."

"Well, you better get going if you plan to have breakfast."

"Yeah, you're right. See you later, honey".

I gave my better half a kiss, went to the garage, jumped into my golf cart, and zipped over to the clubhouse.

As I pulled up to the practice area, a friend, Bob Clark, yelled out, "Hey, Andy, the albacore are biting. Let's go fishing."

"Sounds good to me. You want to charter the *Patriot*?"

"Sounds like a plan. I'll make the arrangements after our round."

Later that evening, the phone rang. Bob said, "It's all set up. I talked to Greg (captain of the *Patriot*) and booked a two-day trip, a week from Monday. Okay with you?"

"It's good with me. You talk to anybody else?"

"Yeah, looks like Ed Cuff, Terry Small, and Bill Hasvold can go. You have anybody else in mind"?

"Yeah, I'll call my cousin, Joe Zitko, and my nephew, John Wright; they're good fisherman and a lot of fun. I'll also call a good friend of mine, John Chuka, who I'm sure would love to go. That would bring it to eight good fishermen"

Both John and Joey called back to confirm. The plan was for all four of us to meet at my house in San Pedro, Monday afternoon, and take my Land Rover to H&M Landing, in San Diego. The rest of our party was driving in Murrieta, about sixty miles from the landing. We planned to rendezvous at a restaurant near the landing for cocktails and dinner, then get aboard the *Patriot*.

By two o'clock, we were all at my house. We decided to take two cars, because we had so much gear. We loaded up my SUV and John's truck and took off, hoping to miss the rush-hour traffic. We got lucky. It took about three hours to get to the landing, which was full of action. Albacore fever was rampant.

Albacore are not only considered one of the best tasting fish, but a great fighter, challenging any angler. When the word got out that the albacore were biting, the landing reservation phones rang off the hook, and whatever boats had not been previously chartered, would soon be booked. When we arrived, all the parking lots were full. There were people all over the place. Some were arriving and anxious to board their boats and go fishing. Others were getting off the boats, finishing their single to multi-day trips, fishing both U.S. and Mexican waters.

First thing, get a parking spot! The place was like a circus with fisherman and looky-loos running around, and cars jockeying for a parking spot. If we were lucky, a boat or two might drop off their passengers, who would eventually find their cars. If not, it could take over an hour to park. We got lucky. Two cars pulled out, and we slid right in.

Joey asked me, "When are we meeting for dinner?"

"At six. We've got twenty minutes; let's go check out the action."

We left our gear locked up in my Land Rover and headed for the dock. The aroma of smoked tuna filled the air. The dock was like a beehive of people, with four boats pulling in and their fisherman milling around the dock. When their trip started, each angler received a number, and any fish he caught was immediately tagged for identification at the end of the trip.

The crews loaded carts full of fish and pushed them up to the dock. Each boat had its own staging area, where the passengers circled and waited for the crew to call out their numbers.

There was total chaos. The crew members yelled out numbers, the fishermen claimed their fish and dragged them into piles. There were booths set up around the staging area with vendors selling handpacked, canned, or smoked albacore, and trying to convince the fishermen to trade their fresh tuna for the cans or smoked fish. I felt either way the fishermen got the worst part of the deal, but if they preferred smoked, or canned fish, instead of fresh, who was I to criticize.

We walked around and took in the action. Joey said, "Hey, Chuka, looks like the fishing couldn't be better."

"Man, I'm glad I could make it. I almost had to cancel because of a real estate deal. You know, I didn't have time to change my fishing line. It's only a couple of years old, so it should be OK, don't you think?"

"Are you kidding? I changed my line, just for this trip. Wouldn't you get pissed if your line broke every time you hooked a big fish?"

"I guess I better get some new line."

"John and I filled our reels on Wednesday at the Rusty Hook. I think you need to pay a visit to the tackle store."

We wandered over to the H&M Landing store where John bought the line he needed, and the rest of us were able to find something new to add to our tackle boxes.

We got to the restaurant about 6:00 P.M. The rest of the group was waiting for us at the bar. We had just ordered a drink when the hostess informed us that our table was ready. Dinner was fantastic, we all drank too much and had a great time. We were all pumped up to go fishing, and then the stories started: *How I lost the big one.*

"Joey, remember when we were at the East Cape, near Cabo San Lucas and caught seven marlin in two hours?"

"How about that time when the four of us caught 290 albacore in one day!" said Bob.

"Yeah, sure, take off the zero, and I might believe you," said Bill.

Red Sky Morning

"Hey, Bob, did you get a scar where Bill hooked you in the ass?"

Everybody was laughing, then they started the heckling. "Ah, come on and show us," yelled Ed.

To our surprise, Bob stood up and browned us all.

That really started things going. Known for his quick wit, Joey jumped in with one of his classic jokes:

"One day, this parish priest, decided to go fishing at the local lake. He got to the marina early in the morning and rented a row boat, loaded up his gear, and rowed out onto the lake. It wasn't long before he caught a fish. He thanked God, took out the hook, and put the fish in a bucket. When he bent over he saw that there was some water in the bottom of the boat. He didn't remember seeing any water before he left the dock, but he wasn't sure.

"He hooked another fish and was reeling it in when another boat with fisherman came by. They congratulated him and noticed a lot of water in the bottom of the priest's boat. One of the fishermen said, 'It looks like you might have a leak,' and offered assistance. The priest responded, 'it's ok. God will keep me safe. Bless you, and good luck.'

"Fishing was red hot, and within the next hour the priest caught five more fish. Another boatload of anglers came by, and one of them asked the priest what kind of bait he was using, then noticed that the priest's boat was around half full of water and again offered him assistance. The priest thanked him but again said, 'God is with me and will take care of his disciples.'

"About fifteen minutes later, a helicopter flew over the lake and hovered over the priest. The pilot called down and offered assistance. The priest's response was the same.

Later the priest decided to call it a day and started rowing back to the marina, but he didn't get very far before his boat sank and he drowned.

"Now, the priest was in front of St. Peter demanding to speak to God. In front of God, he asked, 'Why have you done this to me? I have been loyal to you, celibate, and have preached your message. Why have you forsaken me?'

"God shook his head, 'What more do you want from me? I sent you two boats and a helicopter!'

Most of the people in the restaurant were cracking up and asking for more. Joey obliged them.

"Down in Louisiana, at Lake Onoke, Ruby and Pearly May, were out fishing for catfish. Pearly May screamed, 'yee, I got another one!'

"Ruby looked at her in disgust, 'Pearly May, we go fishing together all the time, and you seem to always catch more fish than me. What's your secret?'

'Well, Ruby, when I get up in the morning to go fishing, I lift up the covers and take look at Rufus's tool When it's laying on the right side, I fish there, and when it's laying on the left, I fish on that side.'

'Well, tell me, Pearly May, what do you do when it's standin' straight up?'

'Hell, Ruby, I don't go fishing that day.'

We were cracking up when Bob announced that it was 9:30 and time to get on the boat.

We got back to our vehicles, picked up our gear, and headed for the dock. We were going down the ramp, and we could see the *Patriot* at its mooring. Greg and his crew were busy getting ready. Greg spotted us and said, "You picked a great time to go. We slaughtered'em today."

I asked Greg, "How far out were they fishing?"

"About a six-to-seven hour run, and it's a little rough out there"

The *Patriot* was sixty-five feet long, looked more like a yacht than a conventional sportfishing boat, and had a flat deck from bow to stern. It had a large cockpit in the stern, and was big enough to house a large bait tank and eight to ten fishermen. The cockpit connected to the galley area and forward towards the bow were the sleeping quarters. Below the galley's deck was the engine room, housing two big V8 Cummings diesel engines and a generator. She cruised at twelve knots, with a top speed of around eighteen.

The crew of the *Patriot* consisted of the captain, Greg Tasaro and the two deck hands, Dave and Steve. Dave was also an outstanding chef and would be doing the cooking on this trip. Bob and I had been out with this group before, and we knew we were in good hands.

Greg started the engines, and the deck hands let the lines go. Greg backed the *Patriot* out of its mooring steered into the harbor. Next stop was the bait receivers, where we would load up enough live bait to last for two days. It took about ten minutes to get to the receivers.

Greg pulled the *Patriot* next to the bait receivers, and Dave and Steve secured the lines. Greg jumped over to the receiver, which is basically a barge with flotation tanks on the outside, leaving the majority of the center open to the water. The openings have fishing net attached to the sides and bottom. The pen hangs down about ten to fifteen feet, which provides a storage area for the live bait, which is delivered to the receiver by a commercial fishing boat.

The bait looked great with huge anchovies and small sardines in the receivers. Dave picked up a large scoop net attached to a long pole. He scooped from the receiver and passed it over to Steve, who dumped the bait into the *Patriot's* bait tanks. The bait was lively and perfect in size.

Greg fired up the big diesel engines, and the crew untied the lines, then started scrubbing down the deck by the bait tanks.

The captain pushed the throttles forward, starting our run out to the fishing grounds. Albacore migrate up the coast, requiring one or two day trips out of San Diego to locate them. The prized fish shows up in Mexican waters around June, with the bulk of fish moving into the area in August and September. By October, albacore are being caught near Morro Bay and continue moving out into the Pacific.

The fishing areas will change due to ocean currents, water quality, temperature, and the quantity of bait for them to feed on. Albacore can move from an area over-night, so the skippers stay in constant radio contact.

The skipper wasn't lying when he said the ocean was pretty rough. When we got outside the harbor, the boat was rockin' and rollin'. We were all trying to get some sleep, but it was so rough that it was difficult to stay in the bunk. I thought the fishing better be damn good, because the weather sucked. By daybreak, I hoped the ocean would calm down at least enough to stand up and start fishing.

Each of us had brought four to six fishing rods and reels, and lots of fishing tackle. The following is a description of the gear we brought on board. One large trolling rig, consisting of a short, heavy-duty rod with roller guides and a large, quality reel like a Penn International two-speed loaded with fifty-to-eighty pound test monofilament line. On this rig, we tied on a feather jig with a hundred and twenty-pound test leader. The jigs varied in design and color, and we would know in a short time which ones worked the best. The other rods and reels varied in size, based on the weight of the monofilament line. The lightest rig would have fifteen-to-twenty pound test line on its reel. The next, thirty-pound, then forty then fifty. We tied a hook onto each line, so they would be ready to use when we got into some fish.

It was 5:30 in the morning, and I was the first to get on deck. The sun was beginning to peek over the horizon, its rays reflected against the clouds, turning the sky into a fiery red glow. Dave came out of the galley and handed me a cup of coffee.

"Thanks, what a beautiful sunrise."

"That it is; but it could mean a storm is coming. You've heard the old saying, 'Red sky at night, sailor's delight; Red sky morning, sailor's warning'."

"Yeah, but that's not always true."

"Well, the weather's pretty shitty, so don't be surprised if it doesn't get worse."

The captain yelled down from the bridge, "Time to start trolling. Dave, would you bring me up a cup of coffee."

Most of the guys were now on deck, getting their gear set up.

"It's really shitty out there. I hope it calms down a little, or we're going to be in for a long day," said Terry.

I thought of what Dave had said earlier, and hoped that his prediction was wrong.

The *Patriot* had four rod holders, equally spaced across the stern. This meant that there was only room for four of us to troll at one time. We drew cards to pick the order of our turn. The *Patriot's* cruising speed was around fourteen knots. Trolling speed is around seven to eight knots, and Greg started to slow down, then yelled, "Let 'em go."

The first group included Joey, Ed, Bob and my nephew John. They all started to let their line out behind the boat. The best way to troll is to have the outside rigs set their jigs farther out than the center ones. Each jig was set at a different length from thirty to a hundred feet behind the boat. By staggering the jigs, there was less chance of getting tangled, and it was the optimum method to catch fish.

I could feel the excitement on the boat. We were always on watch for a fish to strike, and we would also scan the ocean for circling birds, kelp patties, and porpoise, all of which could have a school of fish beneath them.

When a fish struck, the line would peel off the reel, and we would yell, "HOOKUP!" A lot of things happened at once. The skipper would bring the boat to a stop as fast as he could, and we would grab the rigs that had no fish on, and reel in the empty lines. This would leave the one lucky guy fighting one of the prized game fish in the ocean.

While all this was going on, the deck hand would scoop out some bait and throw it over the side in hope of attracting the school of fish to the boat. We would stow the trolling gear, grab one of the bait rigs, hook up a sardine, and cast it into the chum line. Nothing is more exciting than to see a school of albacore charging the boat, gobbling up the entire chum line.

If we're lucky, everyone gets hooked up, and then it's mad chaos. The fish pull in different directions, and everyone has to be alert or get tangled up. You might hear, "Over you, or under you," and with an experienced group like ours, this was all second nature, and we rarely had any problems. The next thing you'd hear is one of us calling for a gaff, (a long pole with a big hook affixed to one end). The deck hand would grab one, reach over the side, snag the fish, and pull it on board.

About fifteen minutes went by, and Ed screamed, "Hookup!" We all went through the drill, had the live bait in the water as fast as we could, but no takers. Ed fought his fish and reeled it up to the stern where Steve gaffed it, and it was flopping all over the deck. First blood, a nice albacore over thirty pounds. This really got us excited, and Greg got the boat to trolling speed. We were on our way.

In the first two hours, we only had jig strikes, which are better than nothing, but we were still hoping to attract a school to the boat, so we could catch more fish. We were all on the stern talking it up.

Bob was saying that you never know what type of fish or size you might catch when you're trolling.

"You could hook up a big-eye tuna, that could weigh 150 pounds or more, or we might get into some bluefin. Greg said they'd caught a few a couple of days ago, and they averaged thirty to fifty pounds."

A second later, I saw the portside rod double over. "Hook up!"

It was Bob's turn. He grabbed his rod, and we started reeling in the empty lines. I took two turns on the reel, and I hooked up. It caught me by surprise, and the fish damn near pulled the rod out of my hands. About two seconds later, John also hooked up. There were fish everywhere. By the time we reeled in the jig fish, everyone else had hooked up.

Steve was keeping a steady chum line going, throwing anchovies off the rear starboard corner. All we had to do is cast our bait into the chum line, and a fish would grab it.

Dave and Greg were gaffing the fish as soon as we got them to the surface and next to the boat. Sometimes, the hook was too hard to get out, so we cut the line (this was the time that having extra bait rigs came in handy), stow that rod, and grab another. The fishing was great, but it could stop just as fast as it started. There was fish and blood all over the deck. Everybody was yelling and whooping. This is what fishing's all about. Then it happened; the bite came to a screeching halt.

"Well, it's time to start trolling again," said Greg, moving up to the bridge. He put the *Patriot* in gear, and we were on our way. Steve was stowing the fish in a netted area on the stern's swim step, and Dave was washing down the deck. Steve yelled out, "We got twenty-seven fish on that stop, and six jig fish earlier, for a total of thirty-three albacore, and it's only eight o'clock in the morning."

"It doesn't get much better that this," said Bill. All of us agreed.

The trolling rigs were out, and we were back watching and searching for more fish. Dave called out, "Anybody for breakfast"?

I said, "I'm ready. What you cooking?"

"Ham and eggs, or a breakfast burrito"

"I'll take a burrito."

Within two minutes, everybody had placed their order, and in ten minutes the food started coming. I took one bite of my burrito, when John yelled out, "Hookup!"

The food got tossed aside, and we went into our drill. It was Terry's turn, and he brought in a nice albie, but there was no further action.

Back to trolling and eating our now cold breakfast, we settled in for the hunt. Dave spotted a kelp patty, and Greg steered toward it. When we got close, Greg slowed down and got within casting distance to the kelp. We all cast bait toward the kelp, Joey immediately hooked up, and so did Bob. Joey said, "It's a small yellowtail."

He had it on the deck in two minutes. Bob's was a little bigger, and Steve had to gaff it. That was it, so the jigs were put out.

Trolling can get a little boring, especially when you don't get a strike for over two hours. No strikes, no kelp, no signs of any fish. We decided it might be a good time to make some changes. We pulled in the lines, I replaced mine with a cedar plug, and John did the same. The rest of the guys tied on new jigs of different styles and colors. We were now ready to get into some action!

Another hour went by, and there wasn't any action, but something smelled good and it was coming from the galley. It had to be lunch, and I was starving. Even if I wasn't hungry, it was something else to do besides sit and wait.

Red Sky Morning

Dave had prepared a delicious Mexican buffet, consisting of fresh yellowtail tacos, carne asada or chicken for burritos or tostadas, and lots of beans and rice. He also whipped up his own hot sauce, and if that wasn't hot enough, there was a dish of jalapeños and serrano chilies that would make you sweat. We finished off the meal with some ice-cold Coronas.

Steve went up to the bridge to relieve Greg so he could have lunch. We were all talking about the action we had that morning, and how exceptionally slow the fishing got as the day went on. Bob asked Greg if he had any ideas to improve the fishing for the afternoon. He said he had decided to leave the area we were fishing that morning and run about twenty-five miles south. He changed course around 10:00 A.M., and we would be in the area in fifteen minutes.

Bob said, "That's why we like to go out with you; you're always on top of it."

Ed offered up some Cohibas, and he had a few takers. We went out on the deck with a fresh Corona, and lit up the cigars. Taking a puff, Joey said, "What more could you ask for?"

"I agreed, "This is great. Now we only need a little more action."

"It wouldn't hurt if it also calmed down a little bit," said Bill.

Bill was right. The wind was picking up, it was getting a little choppy, and the swells were getting bigger.

We heard Greg yell out, "Bring in the lines. I see a lot of birds and fish boiling under them."

We started reeling in the jigs, and I could feel the *Patriot* picking up speed. I had the jig in, stowed the rod, and went up to the bridge to see what was going on. Bob was already there and saw me coming up the ladder.

"Hey, Andy, take a look at this." Bob handed me some

binoculars, and I could see a lot of birds working an area off the bow, and the fish jumping.

"Hey Greg, what kind of tuna?"

"I think they're bluefin. Tell the guys to get ready, and to use forty-pound test or heavier. I think we're going to run into some big fish."

We were closing in on the school, and Greg slowed down. Steve got up on the bait tank, grabbed the scoop net, and got ready to chum. We drifted into the middle of the tuna and Greg yelled, "Start chumming"

The tuna immediately started boiling on the bait, I hooked a sardine, and cast it out toward the boils. A tuna rolled over my bait but didn't take it. My nephew yelled, "Hookup!" and I could see he had a big fish on. Another tuna boiled on my bait, but this time he took it. I let him take out some line, I put the reel in gear and set the hook. I had decided to use my fifty-pound-test rig, and after setting the hook, I was glad I did. This was a big fish. It was pulling out my line, and I had the drag set as tight as possible.

John and I were the first to hook up, and within two minutes, all our rods were doubled over. Greg couldn't resist, and cast a bait over the side. It was instantly struck. Greg yelled, "Hey, Dave, we're going to have sashimi tonight".

"Sushi, sashimi, spicy tuna roll, we'll have it all".

While talking about dinner, Dave bent over the side and gaffed John's fish. With a big grunt, Dave pulled one whopping bluefin tuna over the rail.

"Damn, that's got to be over fifty pounds".

"Way to go, John," yelled Joey."

"Hey, Andy, what's taking so long?"

"He's not budging. Every time I reel in ten feet, he takes twenty. Shit, I've got over a hundred and fifty yards out, and I can't stop him."

Red Sky Morning

While I hung on, a few more tuna came over the side. Most of the fish averaged thirty-five to forty pounds. Dave gaffed Greg's fish and left it flopping on the deck. Greg stowed his rod, grabbed another gaff and went to work. A half-hour went by, and almost everybody had a fish on.

Joey was on his third. He yelled, "Under you." I backed off the rail, and let Joey go under my pole. As he went by, he asked, "Are you gaining on him"?

"Yeah, a little"

Everybody was yelling and whooping. Bill bellowed, "I've never experienced anything like this. This fish is kicking my ass!" He was right; bluefin tuna, pound for pound, are among the toughest fish in the ocean.

The bite was slowing down, and I was gaining some line. I had been fighting this fish for close to an hour, when I finally could see its color. I had maybe fifty feet of line out, and I could see that it was one big sucker. The next thirty feet seemed to take forever to reel in, and I now realized just how tired I was. Greg looked over the side and announced, "You got a Bigeye." The tuna was getting close to the surface; both Greg and Dave had gaffs over the side. I'm a big guy, and in pretty good shape, but my arms were shaking, and my shoulders and back were killing me.

Greg got the first gaff in and hung on until Dave's gaff was securely hooked, then they pulled that Bigeye over the side. I was ecstatic, and everyone was congratulating me. I asked Greg, "So what do you think?"

"I think it's a hundred and fifty, maybe more."

All I could say was, "WOW!"

"Well, you guys have enough for today, or should we keep fishing?" barked the captain.

John said, "You never know what tomorrow's going to be like, so lets keep going."

Of course we all agreed, so throttle forward, jig lines

out, and off we went.

We had a couple of good jig stops, and caught a few more albacore. Then we picked up some nice size yellowtails by a kelp patty. There was some dolphin (Mahi Mahi) mixed in with the yellows, and we got a few of them.

By four in the afternoon, we had over a hundred fish on board. We were totally exhausted and decided to call it a day. When you're on a two-day trip, and over a hundred miles out to sea, you spend the second night drifting with a sea anchor out. A sea anchor really isn't an anchor like you see hanging off the bow of a boat, but a weighted nylon parachute, that when let out, opens under water.

When the sea anchor is set up properly, it helps stabilize the boat and slows down the drift, so the boat's position doesn't change drastically. As it began to get dark we hoped the weather would improve, but the wind and the swells appeared to be picking up again, which meant another uncomfortable night of bouncing around in your bunk.

We all took turns taking showers and got dressed for dinner, which meant putting on clean shorts and a T-shirt. One by one, we filed into the galley, where Dave was working on dinner. He had already prepared a platter of sushi and sashimi from a fillet of bluefin that Dave cut up earlier. The drinks were flowing, and the appetizers were delicious. Joey brought a half-gallon of VO onboard, and when everybody else put their favorite booze on the table, it looked like a commercial bar. Joey offered me a VO and soda, which I gladly accepted.

We were all talking about the great day of fishing we had when Greg entered the galley. He was greeted with a cheer and a toast to a successful day. We all had a drink to the day's success. Then, Greg got roasted by Bob, and I. We started telling jokes, and Joey got on a roll. Everybody was laughing and just having a hell of a time.

Red Sky Morning

"Dinner's ready," yelled Dave.

"I don't know how in the hell you can cook anything in this weather," said Terry.

"It's not easy, but tonight we have Caesar salad, rack of lamb, stir-fried vegetables, and a few bottles of Cabernet, compliments of Bob."

Dinner was excellent, and after dessert we settled down with a cappuccino, cognac, or some aged port from my wine cellar. Cigars were passed around. There wasn't any reception on the TV, and we had watched all the current videos the night before.

John asked," Anybody want to play gin"?

"How much a point?" asked Terry.

"How about ten cents."

"Count me in."

"Me too," said Bill, and Joey.

It was really windy, and the waves were knocking us around. It became hard to keep your balance, so everybody sat down and hung on. We played cards for a while, but it didn't seem that anybody was too interested. Ed started telling a story about a long range fishing trip he was on, and the bad weather they ran into.

"The waves were breaking over the bow, and most of the people were sick. There's no way you could get comfortable in your bunk, so a lot of us hung out in the galley. They were a long way from shore, heading home from the Clarion Islands, so they had to just weather the storm. By the next morning, the weather calmed down some, and the skipper went out to assess the damage. We had lost one life raft off the top of the bridge. That meant some of the waves must have been fifteen to twenty feet. I asked the skipper about it and he said, he didn't want to alarm any of us, but there was a point when he didn't think we were going to make it."

Ed wrapped up his story, then Bob shared an experience he had on a trip that was equally as exciting, in fact it topped Ed's story, because they lost a passenger overboard.

"I mean someone saw him fall overboard and notified the skipper, who slowed down and turned around to look for him. We searched for over an hour. The skipper came down to talk to us, and had tears in his eyes."

He said, "I guess we lost him. Shit, I've never had anything like this happen."

"The skipper poured himself a cup of coffee and sat down, then he began to cry, and so did many of us. God, you never know when your time's up."

Joey jumped in, "Back in the '40s and '50s, my father was a commercial fisherman. He worked on the *Liberator*, out of San Pedro. The *Liberator* was an 85-foot purse seiner, and most of the crew were Croatian and related. They were fishing for tuna off the coast of Mexico.

"Fishing was really good, and there were five other boats working the same area. In those days, they used celestial navigation and communicated by short-wave and ship-to-shore radios with limited range. If the weather got bad, they would head for shelter in a bay or the lee side of an island. This day they were caught off guard, and a *chubasco* slammed right into them. My dad said the waves were over forty feet, and the wind blew so hard that the sea whipped up a layer of foam over a foot thick. They were a long way from shore, so they had no choice but to ride out the storm. By the next morning, they had lost their skiff, their net, and most of the gear secured on deck. Another boat, the *Pacific Dawn*, started having problems shortly after nightfall.

"The other captains heard the skipper call for assistance, because they were taking on water and starting to sink. All the boats were having their own problems, but they still tried to locate her. "Twenty minutes later, the

Red Sky Morning

skipper was yelling, "Mayday, Mayday!" There was a pause, then he cried out, "Oh God help us!" That night the *Pacific Dawn* sunk. There were no survivors.

"Another boat, the *Rosa Marie,* lost her mast, and while they were trying to secure the rigging, two of the crew were washed overboard, never to be seen again. Many of these fishermen were related, and a lot of brothers and cousins lost their lives. In fact, my dad lost his cousin, who worked on the *Pacific Dawn*. I'll tell you, those guys led a tough life."

John was pouring another glass of port and said, "I read that commercial fishing was rated the most dangerous profession in the world. My 'Dida', grandfather to you non-Croatians, told me a few stories that convince me. Hey, Andy, why don't you tell them what happened to you when you went fishing with "Dida" while you were a senior in high school."

Bob interrupted, "Yeah, you told me part of that story last time we went fishing. It's quite a story. I'd like to hear the rest."

"It's a long story, but I've been told it would make a great movie and that I should write a book about it. As a matter of fact, I started writing the book about a month ago."

"Well, you might as well start from the beginning," said Terry, "because you've got a captive audience. I'm ready for a good story, and I know damn well, none of us are going to get any sleep in this shitty weather.

"Well, here it goes."

"Does the book have a name"? asked Ed.

"Well it didn't until last week, when my wife named it *Red Sky Morning.*

Chapter 2

Summer vacation was going to start tomorrow. I was a senior in high school and would be graduating in the winter class of 1964. I was sitting in my history class, daydreaming about surfing and partying all summer. I was on a big wave, hanging ten, at my favorite surfing spot, when I heard a familiar voice calling my name. "Andy."

I realized I was daydreaming, and I was still in class. My girlfriend, Jan, was standing in front of me, smiling. "Didn't you hear the bell? School's out. Let's get out of here."

Walking down the hall, Jan asked, "When are you going to pick me up?"

We were going to a big party that night, and Jan knew that my hot rod—a 1934 Ford three-window coupe—wasn't running because the transmission had blown while drag racing the previous Saturday night.

"Well, you know"

"Yeah, I know, but why don't you get a normal car, so we don't have to bum a ride from one of your friends?"

I was getting the hint. I could screw off all summer, and Jan would probably break up with me, or I could get a job, make some money, and buy a new car. I really liked Jan, but to miss out on all the fun? This was a big decision for me, but I guess it was time to grow up a little. Shit, there goes the summer.

I've always had a summer job. When I was a kid, I delivered papers, mowed lawns, whatever it took to make a few bucks. When I turned thirteen, I got job as second deck hand, on my neighbor's charter fishing boat, the *Bolo*. Roy Creal was my neighbor, and his son, Roy Jr., was the first deckhand and one of my friends. The *Bolo* was thirty-eight feet long, and was moored at Twenty-second Street Landing in San Pedro. The boat was chartered almost every day during the summer. It was hard work, but we got to fish once in a while, in fact I learned a lot about sport fishing and running a boat that summer.

For the next four summers, I worked on various boats at the landing. Some were charter boats, and the others were open party boats, operated by the landing. I loved it. In fact, when I had a day off I went fishing. I just couldn't get enough of it. But this summer, I was a senior, and all I wanted to do was go surfing, party, and be with my girlfriend. I still planned to go fishing a lot, and I knew I could go for free anytime. Well, it really wasn't totally free. I would go out as a "deadhead," a boating term that meant you could go fishing free, but you had to help clean up the boat on the way in. It was a good trade-off, and my family always had fresh fish for dinner.

Speaking about my family, I have a great family. My father is a commercial fisherman, and my mother takes care of the house, my sister, and me. Our extended family is huge, and they almost all live in San Pedro.

My grandparents, my mother, and many of my aunts and uncles emigrated from the Dalmatian Coast, now known as Croatia. Most of them were fisherman, merchant seamen, or worked in the shipyards. My mother, her sister, and my grandmother, immigrated to the U.S. in 1933. My grandfather came to the United States in 1922 and stayed with family in Hokum, Washington.

His desire was to save enough money to eventually bring his family to the U.S. He first worked in a lumberyard, and than became a commercial fisherman. Reunited with his wife and children, he moved to San Pedro, where his wife, Tonia, had their third daughter.

He invested in a new fishing boat with his relatives. His family emigrated from an island called Dugi Otok, which meant Long Island, and the partners felt their new boat deserved the same name, the *Long Island*. My father was born in Bainbridge, Washington, where his father was a commercial fisherman.

Shortly after my dad was born, the family moved to San Pedro, where my grandfather became partner on another boat, where he worked until he retired. My father also became a commercial fisherman, met my mother, and eventually married her. He saved his money and bought out the cook's ownership of the *Long Island*, and eventually became the captain.

Commercial fishing was a tough life. It was hard work, long hours, and could be dangerous. In those days, they fished primarily for sardines and the seasonal local run of tuna. The fleet fished for sardines from the coast off San Diego to San Francisco. My father became President of the Fisherman's Association, which meant more work and time away from the family.

My sister, Karen, was born in 1943, and I came into the world in 1946. Shortly after, my father became partners in another boat the *Sea Scout*, a ninety-foot purse seiner, which was built with family money, and the crew was all related. My dad became the captain, whereupon he and his crew ventured out to take advantage of the growing sardine industry.

The birth of the sardine industry was in Monterey, California, in the early 1900s. There was an abundant supply of sardines in Monterey Bay, but the crude method of fishing limited the quantity of fish caught.

An Italian fisherman named Pete Ferrante immigrated to Monterey and introduced a new method of fishing using a lampara net, which was being used back in Italy. The lampara is a net that will encircle an entire school of fish, enabling the fish to be pulled to the lampara boat, where the fishermen would scoop them out of the water and into the hold of their boat.

With the use of the lampara net, the supply of sardines was no longer a problem. By 1918, there were many canneries lined up on the shore, processing the hundreds of tons being delivered by the local fleet. It was during this time that the Monterey waterfront became known as "Cannery Row."

In the late '20s, the half-ring net and half-ring boat were introduced. Many more fish could be caught per haul as the net rings created a purse, thus trapping the fish, making it impossible for them to escape.

By the mid-'30s, the half-ring boats were being replaced by a new vessel called the purse seiner, which got its name from the type of net it carried. Varying in size, the largest were eighty to ninety feet long, and carried nets three to five hundred feet long and sixty to eighty feet in depth. This new type of boat had a range of hundreds of miles, and carried over a hundred tons of fish in its hold.

The sardine industry was flourishing, with 1945 being its best year. This was also when the book, *Cannery Row* by John Steinbeck, was published, immortalizing the Monterey waterfront.

Sardine fishing not only flourished in Monterey, but became one of the largest industries on the West Coast. Not only was there money and employment in fishing and canning, but there were many by-products as well. Fish meal was used for poultry and livestock feed, as well as fertilizer. The oil extracted from the sardine was sought-after for use in manufacturing soap, paint, vitamins, glycerin (for World War II ammunition), salad oil, and more.

San Pedro had its own canneries, processing plants, and fleet of purse seiners. The *Long Island* and the *Sea Scout* were part of that fleet. The fleet not only fished in Southern California's waters, but would go wherever the fishing was most productive. They fished off the coast of San Francisco, unloading their catch at a local cannery, or to offshore floating processing plants.

During WWII, the fishermen were exempt from the draft because of the demand for fish and its by-products. Fishermen were respected and welcomed at any establishment, because they had money and were looking for a good time during their short visits ashore.

In the early '50s, when the volume of sardines started to diminish, no one could explain why. Some said the fish were disappearing, and in fact, the whole industry started to die. Shortly thereafter, the Local Fisherman's Association closed down.

Monterey's sardine industry became little more than a memory. This once-robust industry had a life span of less than fifty years. Why the sardines disappeared remains a mystery. Some say it was because of an increase in pollution, climate change, currents and water temperatures, or maybe they were over-fished into extinction.

With the disappearance of the sardine, the San Pedro fishermen were faced with a major problem. Local tuna fishing was seasonal and not big enough to sustain a boat and its crew. So, it was time to make some changes. There was a lot of tuna to catch in Mexican waters. So, the San Pedro fleet and their crews began to make the necessary changes to adapt to a new way of life.

During the sardine era, the fisherman stayed close to home. When the fish were close to San Pedro, they were in and out of port and had a lot of time to spend with family and friends. Now they would be fishing for tuna in Mexico, which meant they would be spending a lot more time away from home. A trip took from twenty to thirty days, or more.

The fishing industry was changing. Boats were getting larger and had longer range. San Diego became the port for the larger fishing vessels. There were two types of tuna fishing boats at the dock. One was called a bait boat, the other a purse seiner. Bait boats were the first type of long-range fishing boats. Their method of fishing was the toughest of all. First, the boat had to get to the fishing grounds, then they had to catch live bait, and lots of it. Next, they had to find schools of tuna and attract them to the boat by chumming. Then, the fisherman climbed over the rail and onto steel racks and used a long cane poll with a short line attached to the tip and a feather jig on the end. The fisherman would slap the water with the jig, hoping that a tuna would grab it. The fisherman had to be alert, because when a tuna bit, he needed the momentum of the fish to help lift the fish over the rail and onto the deck. It was backbreaking work, and the men never stopped to rest until the fish stopped biting.

Tuna came in all sizes, ranging from five pounds to three hundred pounds. When the big fish were biting, the men would combine two to three lift poles, with one line and one jig. It was amazing to watch three men in perfect sync, pull a 250-pound tuna over the rail.

The San Pedro fleet was all purse seiners and needed to

make a few changes before they ventured into Mexican waters. The small mesh netting used to catch sardines was replaced by a much stronger and larger mesh net, around a hundred to one hundred fifty yards long. They also carried a freezer or two on board to hold more food for the longer trips. All of these boats carried ice, and some had refrigeration systems in the hold, that could carry eighty to a hundred and fifty tons of fish.

The fishing industry was rapidly changing. The bait boats were being replaced or converted to purse seiners. The newly built purse seiners were 150 to 200 feet long, and could hold over 1000 tons of tuna. The tuna was preserved in circulating freezing brine water, which could preserve the fish for a much longer period of time. In order to catch that much fish the boats were equipped with better electronics and machinery, and their nets were over a mile long. Some of the new vessels had a helicopter aboard, which was used to spot schools of fish.

The smaller purse seiners were limited by range and preservation of the tuna and had to compete with the larger boats. The growing worldwide demand for tuna motivated other countries to establish their own fishing fleets. Mexico became very aggressive and developed their own fleet of purse seiners.

The competition was growing, and the smaller boats were being pushed out. To make matters worse for the San Pedro fleet, the local StarKist Tuna cannery announced that it planed to close down, and was building a new facility in Puerto Rico, and possibly one in Guam.

That left three smaller canneries in San Pedro, but it was just a matter of time before the tuna industry was finished locally. StarKist was making this change because the largest fishing grounds proved to be south of Mexico, from Ecuador to Peru.

These changes decimated the local fleet, and many of the fishermen. The Italians and Croatians operated and owned most of the boats, and their crews were all family members. Many chose to leave the fishing industry and work ashore. Some of the owners sold their boats, retired, or bought real estate. Others decided to hang on and fish locally for mackerel, squid, and the seasonal tuna run.

The rest moved on to the large purse seiners. It was no longer a family-type business, but corporate-owned vessels with crews made up of various nationalities. The crews were mostly Hispanic and were not U.S. citizens. They were good seamen, and their pay scale was much lower. Captains, navigators and engineers came from the U.S. They were of Croatian, Italian, and Portuguese descent. My father was one of these fishermen and became captain of the *Jenny Lynn*, out of San Diego. He ran that boat for a couple of years, then became captain of the *Espirito Santos*, which was 130 feet long. A year later, he moved on to a much larger vessel the *Western Ace.*

Chapter 3

School had been out for a couple of days, and the weather and surfing couldn't get much better. My friends and I were surfing at one of our favorite spots, Royal Palms. The waves were head-high and had perfect form. We started around seven in the morning and had been in and out of the water all day. Some of the girls, including Jan, drove down to catch some rays and a few waves.

"I see you got your hot rod running. Does that mean you're taking me to the party tonight?" said Jan.

"Yeah, Roy had some extra transmission gears, and we worked on my car till midnight, and absolutely yes to the party."

She sounded a little pissed off, but I didn't think this was a good time to ask her why. Anyway, the girls decided to leave. I no longer had to pay attention to Jan, so I went out to catch a few more waves.

It was around three in the afternoon, and I decided to go home. I was just about to turn into our driveway when I saw my dad coming up the street from the other direction. Well, this is his house and his right of way, so I waited for him to pull into the garage then parked behind him.

"So, how's the jalopy running"?

"It's running great. The gears are a little tight, but they'll break in."

"I hope they have a chance to break in before you break them".

We both laughed and walked into the house together.

"You start looking for a job yet"

"No, but I think it's about time to get serious about it. Hey, Dad, how long you gonna be home?"

"I have a few things to go over with the owners of the boat, then I'll be leaving. Probably in a week or so".

My father had just got home last week. As the captain of the *Western Ace,* he's gone a lot more. His trips usually last between thirty-forty days, fishing for tuna off the coasts of Ecuador and Peru. When they finally loaded up with tuna, the boat sailed to Puerto Rico to unload the fish at the new StarKist cannery.

To reach Puerto Rico, the boat had to go through the Panama Canal and in Panama, my father turned over the helm to the second mate and flew home. This gave him more time at home, usually around two or three weeks.

During dinner that night, my dad explained what he and the owners had to meet about. The captains, and owners of six big purse seiners had decided to make a run up the East Coast of the U.S., to fish the summer season run of tuna. This was going to be the first time this size and type of vessel had made an attempt to fish in that area.

Some of the boats were on their way to Puerto Rico to unload their catch, one of which was the *Western Ace.* Two of the boats were already at the StarKist cannery, waiting to unload. It appeared that they could travel up the East Coast together.

We finished dinner and moved to the den to watch some TV. Dad turned on the news. BORING!

Red Sky Morning

I decided to call Jan and plan out the evening. The party was at some girl's house, and her parents were on vacation, so we needed to buy some beer. None of us had fake IDs, but at six foot three and two hundred and fifty pounds, I can usually pass for twenty-one.

I picked up Jan at eight, and we met our friends in a liquor store parking lot, where I collected the money, went in, and bought two cases of beer. Now we were ready to rock' n' roll. By the time we got to the party, Jan and I had already downed a six-pack. The party was jumping, and we knew almost everyone there. Things were going great until a bunch of guys came in that weren't familiar. They looked like a bunch of dopers, not that most of us haven't smoked some pot, but these guys appeared to be on some heavy shit.

These assholes started wrecking the house and started a fight with one of my friends. It was getting ugly, and I felt sorry for the girl throwing the party. One of the dopers almost knocked Jan down, so I grabbed the SOB by the neck and threw him on the floor. He came up swinging, but I blocked his punch and decked him. One of his friends saw me hit him, and came at me. I dodged his attempt nailed him squarely on the jaw, and he went down on top of his buddy.

It was time to get the hell out of there. I grabbed Jan, who looked stunned, and headed for the door. I was just opening Jan's door when the first cop car rounded the corner.

They stopped right next to us, then two more black-and-whites stopped at the house. One cop jumped out and asked, "What's going on?"

I was scared shitless. I'd had a lot to drink and had a pretty good buzz going. I carefully said, "We were invited here but some guys crashed the party and started to wreck the house. I decided to get out of there."

He must have noticed something and asked, "Have you been drinking?"

I told him I had a couple of beers earlier and felt fine. He didn't agree and made me walk the curb. I slipped off twice. *Man am I in trouble.*

The cop laughed and said, "I don't think it would be wise for you to drive. Where do you live?"

I told him, and he asked for my keys. "Let's go. You come with me, and my partner and your girlfriend will follow us to your house."

I thought I was in deep shit, and my parents would be really pissed. Shit, I could lose my license. The officer asked me what my name was, and he said he was familiar with my family. *This is great. In a couple of minutes the cop and I will be standing at my front door talking to my father. Shit.*

He pulled my hot rod into the drive way and turned off the ignition.

"Nice car. Did you build it?"

"From scratch."

We got out of the car, he walked over to my side, and handed me my keys. "Don't ever let me catch you trying to drive in your condition." He started for the patrol car. "You're lucky I'm in a good mood tonight. We'll take your girlfriend home. Go to bed. Good night".

I couldn't believe it; he let me off the hook. It was a little early for me to be coming home, but maybe my parents were asleep and wouldn't notice the time. I opened the door and the lights were off. So far, so good. I got to my bedroom, shut the door, and herd my mother ask, "How come you're home so early?" I didn't know what to say, so I told her that Jan and I had a fight, and she wanted to go home. Mom said, "That's too bad. Good night".

Red Sky Morning

I couldn't get to sleep. I was too wound up, so I just lay there and thought about tonight's experience. I couldn't believe I got away with it. *God, I wonder how Jan is.* I couldn't call her house this late, so it would have to wait.

It was like two in the morning, and I was thinking about where I wanted to work this summer. I knew I could go to work on a sportfishing boat, but I really didn't want to. Then it came to me. How about going fishing with my father? He said the tuna season was during the summer, which meant I could make it. Nah, Mom would never go for it, and why would I think my dad would approve. Well, I decided it wouldn't hurt to ask, so I planned to see what they would say in the morning.

It was seven in the morning, and I might have got a couple of hours of shuteye. I just couldn't think of anything else but going fishing with my dad. On a forty or fifty-day job. I could make lots of money and still have at least a month of summer to surf and screw around. I couldn't wait to ask. If it was OK with Dad, and I got Mom's blessing, I'd be on my way.

Dad was sitting at the table having a cup of coffee and reading the local paper, which we called the "fish wrapper." Mom was at the stove, fixing breakfast. *It's now or never.* I poured myself a cup of coffee and sat down.

My dad looked over the paper and said, "Good morning son."

I returned the greeting and got right to the subject. "Hey, Dad, you know, I've been thinking about where I should work this summer, and I came up with a really good idea."

"Yeah, so what's your plan?"

"Well, you mentioned that you're going fishing on the East Coast this summer, and I thought you might hire me to work on your boat."

My mother jumped in, "I don't think that's a very good idea. You're too young, and I think you should stay home and work on the sportfishing boats."

"Ah, Honey, he'll be seventeen in a month for Christ's sake, and he's as strong as a horse."

"But how are you going to drop him off the boat when it's time for him to get back to school? I just don't think it's a good idea."

"Just think. He'll be able to see Puerto Rico and the East Coast and spend some time with me. We'll be close to lots of ports where he could leave to come home. He also won't be getting into any trouble, like getting drunk at parties and things like that."

Dad was looking right at me when he said that, and I thought to myself, he's got to be referring to last night. How in the hell did he know what happened? I looked up at him, and he had a smirky smile on his face. I was sure I looked guilty as sin.

"What are you talking about?" Mom asked.

"Ah, nothing. C'mon Honey, it'll be good for him, and me. I could use another hand on the boat."

"Well, we'll talk about it later."

Dad smiled and gave me the OK sign. I gave him a thumbs-up and left the kitchen. I was really surprised when later that day, Mom told me it was OK to go. There was only one more obstacle, my girlfriend, Jan. I intended to go, no matter what, but I thought asking for her approval was the right thing to do. She didn't like it, but she said she understood. So I was off to Puerto Rico! It should be like a great vacation. I hoped.

Chapter 4

Dad and I were all packed and ready to go. Our plane left LAX at 12:55 P.M., and Mom was going to drive us to the airport. We were sitting in the living room, talking about the trip. My dad explained that there had been a change of plans. Just two days ago, the engineer on the boat had slipped and broke his arm. He had to be replaced, and the owner had hired a new man. My father didn't know the guy, but he was to meet us at the airport and travel with us.

It took about forty minutes to get to the airport, so we left the house at eleven. That gave us over an hour before the plane departed. Dad pulled to the curb, and I opened the trunk to unload the luggage. We said our good-byes and headed for the ticket counter, where the new engineer was waiting for us.

My dad said, "Hi, I'm Andy Rafkin, and this is my son, Andy."

He moved to shake the engineer's hand, but the man didn't respond and said, "Yeah, nice to meet you. My name is Ed Johnson." His voice was real raspy, and he was smoking a cigarette. He seemed a little rough around the edges and not my type of guy, but I was sure the owners of the boat knew their business.

We got our tickets and walked to the boarding ramp. *Shit this is the first time I've ever been on a plane.* I was surprised I hadn't thought about it earlier. I guess I was so excited about going that it didn't cross my mind

I couldn't believe it. My dad, his new engineer, and I were boarding a Delta Airlines flight to Puerto Rico via New Orleans. We got to our seats, and Dad let me sit by the window. He sat next to me, and Ed took the aisle seat. Before I knew it, we were in the air. The captain came on the intercom, greeting and thanking us for using Delta Airlines. He informed us about the length of the flight, how high we would be flying, and that the weather looked good for at least half the flight. He went on to say that there was a low-pressure area developing in the Gulf, and the ride might get bumpy later.

Our flight attendant was a fox and really nice. She served us lunch and asked me if I wanted a beer. I took a chance and accepted. Dad didn't say anything and ordered one for himself. Ed was already on his second drink and kept to himself. My dad tried to start a conversation with him, but his answers were short, with little attempt to continue talking. My dad seemed a little annoyed and spoke to me in Croatian. "I don't know about this guy. He's a little strange. You want to play some gin rummy?" I agreed about Ed, and my dad asked the stewardess for a deck of cards.

We were on our fourth game, when the captain's voice came over the speaker, "I hope everyone is enjoying the flight. I wanted to give you an update on that low-pressure system moving in from the Gulf of Mexico. It's nothing to worry about, but we should encounter some rough weather in about twenty to thirty minutes from now. The turbulence

Red Sky Morning

will probably last throughout the rest of the flight. I'm going to turn on the safety belt sign, and I recommend staying in your seats."

My dad kicked my butt in the first two games of gin. We were in the middle of the third game when it started to get a little bumpy, then without warning the plane dropped and shuddered. I looked at my dad He smiled and told me that we had hit an air pocket, and not to worry.

Well, it remained bumpy, and we occasionally hit an air pocket. This was a new experience to me, and a little scary, but I got over it. The captain announced that we were approaching New Orleans, and for the flight attendants to prepare for landing. I looked out the window and could see the lights of the city. It had begun to rain. The landing was a little bumpy, and I tensed up a little. I was relieved when we started to taxi to the docking area.

There was a one-hour layover before we left for Puerto Rico. The plane was departing from Gate Twenty-two, and our baggage was being forwarded. We were walking to our gate and passed a restaurant. My dad asked if I wanted something to eat. I said sure. He asked Ed, who said he wasn't hungry, but was going to get a drink. I was sure it wasn't a Coke.

We were looking at the menu, wondering what to order. "Well, have you decided?" asked my dad. I couldn't make up my mind, and Dad suggested that I might order a big fat hamburger, because I wouldn't be getting another for a while. We both ordered a double cheeseburger with fries and downed it with a chocolate shake. We talked about the rest of the trip. My dad explained that after we arrived in the city of San Juan, we would then take a small plane to our final destination, Ponce, which was a small town located on the other side of the Island. The plane seated ten passengers, and was nothing like the 707 jetliner we were just on. It would be an experience.

Well, the one-hour layover was extended because of the weather. The ticket agent at the gate told my dad that the flight might be cancelled, and that we might have to stay overnight. The next flight was at eleven in the morning, and there was room on the plane.

My dad said, because of the delay we wouldn't make it to Ponce that night, because we would miss the plane out of San Juan. We were either staying in New Orleans, or San Juan. We found a seat by our gate and waited for another announcement. Ed wandered over to where we were sitting and asked Dad what was going on. Before he could explain, the girl at the ticket counter announced that we would be boarding in ten minutes.

"Delta Airlines Flight 456 to San Juan, Puerto Rico, is now boarding at Gate A."

We waited our turn, found our row, and I got the window seat. We taxied out to the runway. Out the window, I could see that it was really windy and raining sheets of water that rippled across the tarmac. This was not a night I would want to be out in, but I'm sure the airlines knew what they were doing.

About ten minutes after we took off, the captain welcomed us aboard and said that due to weather conditions, the seatbelt light would stay on, and to stay in our seats. He explained that the low-pressure area had turned into a tropical depression, but the storm was still far enough away to not worry about.

I asked my dad, "What's a tropical storm? Is it dangerous?"

"A category of a tropical storm, is less than a hurricane, with winds from thirty to sixty miles an hour, and it can be dangerous. If I was out to sea and received a weather report of an oncoming storm of that magnitude, I'd try to avoid it."

Red Sky Morning

This worried me a little, but we were on another 707, and the last one seemed to handle the turbulence pretty good. It was about as rough as the previous flight, but the weather must have gotten worse, because the seatbelt light was flashing, and the plane was starting to bounce all over.

The pilot came on the intercom and said the weather was intensifying, so he had decided to climb above the storm to ease the turbulence. As the plane increased its altitude the turbulence settled down. The flight attendant announced that they were going to start serving dinner, and we had a choice of steak or chicken. We all ordered steak.

We lowered our trays, and the stewardess was pushing the food cart toward us, when suddenly the plane started shaking violently, and than it felt like we were dropping straight down. Shit was flying all over the place, and people were screaming. The nose of the plane dove, and the stewardess loss control of her cart, which rolled down the aisle. It slammed into the bulkhead by the restrooms and fell over, knocking another flight attendant to the floor. The plane was bouncing around like crazy, and the flight attendant was screaming for someone to help her because she was pinned under the cart. I noticed a bright flash of lightning from my window, and it looked so close, I was sure it was going to hit us. The wings were flapping around like they were made of rubber. Now I was really getting scared. I turned towards my Dad, who was looking right at me. He looked really worried and said, "Hang on, son. It'll be OK."

I looked around; it didn't look OK to me. The passengers were panicking, and someone screamed, "Were going to crash." That freaked everybody out. The flight attendants were trying to help, but they were having difficulty standing up. One of the passengers wearing an Army uniform pulled the cart off the stewardess and secured her in a seat.

The turbulence remained constant, and we hit some more air pockets, but nothing like the first one. It caused some of the overhead luggage compartments to open, and stuff was falling out and landing on the passengers. It was really a mess. The flight attendants were doing the best they could, eventually getting the luggage compartments closed, and trying to calm the passengers.

It felt like time stood still, and everything was moving in slow motion. I didn't know how much time had passed since we hit that first air pocket, but it seemed like a lifetime, and I hoped it wasn't the end of mine.

The pilot announced that we were nearing our destination, and that he was starting to descend. Due to this bad weather, we were going to descend at a much steeper rate than usual. The plane took a nosedive, and stuff was flying all over the place. I looked out the window, and the wings were flapping. God, I thought they might break off. I could even hear the fuselage of the plane creaking from the stress.

My dad looked scared, and I thought it was a good time to start praying. A woman was screaming, "Were going to crash!"

More passengers joined in, and I thought it was all over. Then the plane leveled off, and a second later, the wheels hit the landing strip. We bounced pretty hard, and a couple of passengers screamed. I think they thought we were crashing. There were sighs of relief when everyone realized we were on the ground, and everything was OK.

We were walking down the ramp, and my Dad asked me if I was OK. "Yeah, but it scared the hell out of me."

He turned and hugged me, "I was really worried that we wouldn't make it. God, I take you fishing with me and jeopardize your life."

"There's no way this could be your fault. Anyway,

Red Sky Morning

we're on the ground and safe. Where are we going to stay tonight?"

"I think we'll stay at the Intercontinental Hotel. It's close to the airport, and it has a casino and live entertainment. I think we all deserve a nice evening."

We checked into the hotel which reminded me of the big hotels in Las Vegas. We went to our rooms, showered, and got ready for dinner. We hadn't had anything to eat since New Orleans, and we were all hungry. Dad picked the best restaurant in the place. It was pretty late, so there wasn't any problem getting a table.

"Order anything you want," Dad said, waving over a waiter. He ordered a Scotch and soda, and Ed ordered a martini. The waiter asked me what I wanted. I hesitated, and Dad said, "Go ahead," so I ordered a beer. We ordered everything—hors d'oeuvres, salads, and steak and lobster for three.

Before dinner, I was really wired and thought there would be no way that I would get any sleep. But after that great meal, a couple of beers, and a few glasses of wine, I could barely keep my eyes open. Dad and I both decided to pack it in, and Ed said he was going to look around. I'm sure he would be headed to the bar for a few more martinis.

I woke up to the phone ringing. It was my dad. "Good mooring Andy. I called the airport and there's a two-hour delay. I thought we would go to breakfast and take a tour of the city if you like."

"Well, I've never been here, and I might never be back, so I think it's a great idea."

We ate at the hotel, then hailed a taxi. Dad negotiated a flat fee for a four-hour tour. Juan was a lot of fun, spoke a little English, and gave us an excellent tour of the city. Four hours flew by, and it was time to get back to the hotel, find Ed, and check out.

Chapter 5

Ed wasn't too hard to find. He was in the bar nursing a Bloody Mary, and I'm sure a hangover. We got the luggage, and took a cab to the airport. We got to our gate and found that our plane was late. It had rained a little during the morning, and it was still pretty windy. We were booked on a local airline, and I didn't think they kept a very tight schedule, if any. We waited for over an hour, until an announcement was made that it was time to board our flight. I noticed that we were the only people boarding. When we got outside, I realized why. The plane was a six-passenger, twin-engine job, and it looked like a WWII model.

This trip was becoming a real adventure. The flight was a white-knuckler. The weather had calmed down since last night, but in this flying antique, I was surprised it held together. The pilot seemed to be having trouble staying on course, but thank God it was a short flight. He made a decent landing, considering the windy conditions.

There was a car waiting for us, so we threw our luggage in the trunk and drove to the StarKist cannery docks. Ten minutes later, we turned into the StarKist driveway and parked on the dock. I had never seen the *Western Ace* before. It was a lot bigger than the fishing boats docked in San Pedro. I stood there looking at the bow towering over my head.

"So, what do you think?" asked my dad.

"It's really neat dad and a lot bigger than I imagined."

"She's almost 180 feet long. Let's get aboard, and I'll show you around."

We got our luggage and headed for the gangplank. We were met by a guy with his arm in a sling, who I thought must be the engineer.

"Hi Kenny, this is my son Andy."

We shook hands, and my dad asked Kenny, "How's it going?"

"Well, my arm hurts like hell, but other than that everything is fine. At least until this morning when we found out that there's going to be a three-week delay to unload our fish. Frank went over to the cannery office to find out what the hell is going on. He should be back in a few minutes."

You could see that my dad was totally pissed, and so was I, because the balance of my summer vacation had just disappeared.

Well, if I was going to be here all summer, I better plan to make the best of it. My dad gave me a tour of the boat and introduced me to the crew. They all seemed to be pretty decent guys, but I was the skipper's son, so how else would you expect them to act.

Dad was anxious to talk to Frank about the delay, and asked if I was OK. He went to take care of business. I picked up my bag and headed for the crew's quarters to find a bunk. Most of them were already taken but I had three to pick from. I knew I would be spending a lot of time in here, so I took my time and finally decided to pick one next to a porthole. I like fresh air, and the way it smelled in here . . . well, I made sure that the porthole opened, then threw my stuff on the bunk. I wanted to go back on deck and look around, so I decided to unpack later.

Most of the crew came from Costa Rica, and spoke Spanish. A few of them could speak a little English, and I had taken Spanish as an elective in school, so I figured we would be able to communicate.

I was on deck and ran into Carlos, who was the crew foreman. I said hi, and he looked nervous and said, "Oh, hello, Mr. Rafkin, is everything OK"?

I didn't want to be treated like the boss's son, so this was a good time to nip it in the bud.

"Please, call me Andy, and from now on, I'm part of the crew. In fact, you're the foreman, so I work for you."

I stuck out my hand, which he gladly grabbed and kept shaking. He had a strong grip, and his hands were rough and callused. His face was weathered, with deep wrinkles, and his eyes and smile were genuine.

Dad said that most of the crew were in their mid-to-late twenties, But they all seemed older. Commercial fishing was a tough life, and it was apparent that the weather, sun, and hard work had taken its toll.

"You good man, Andy. We going to have some fun. You like to go to town with us tonight?" I accepted and knew that I had made a friend.

Next stop was the galley. The cook was from San Pedro, and had previously worked for my dad. I had met him five or six years ago when my dad ran the *Sea Scout*. His name was John Urlich, he was Croatian, and spoke with a thick accent. He greeted me with an enthusiastic handshake and a hug. He said that the first mate, Frank Maricich, told him I was coming.

"I remember when you used to come on the boat for lunch with your father, when we were unloading fish at the cannery. You grow up, become good-looking young man."

I thanked him and wondered if he really remembered or was just being nice, but it really didn't matter. He seemed like a nice guy, and Dad said he was a great cook. I told John that I liked to cook and maybe I could help him sometime. He answered in Croatian, saying I was welcome any time I liked.

It was the end of the day, and I was leaning on the railing admiring the sunset. I was thinking about how amazing the last two days had been. Starting with my first major trip, first time on a plane, getting caught in a hurricane, could have crashed and burned, and now I was in Ponce, Puerto Rico, on the deck of the *Western Ace*, starting a new job as a commercial fisherman. WOW!

I was deep in thought when Carlos tapped me on the shoulder. "You still want to go to town with us"?

"Absolutely. When are you leaving?"

"As soon as you get ready. Did you ask your father if it's OK to go with us?"

"Si, and he thought it was a good idea."

"Bueno! Hurry up, get ready, and we go."

It took ten minutes to shower and get dressed. When I got on deck, I saw Carlos and three other crew members on the dock, obviously waiting for me. I ran down the ramp and said, "Let's go party."

Carlos said, "First we go to dinner," than he introduced the other guys. There were Juan, Larry, and Chi Chi, who was Puerto Rican, and got his name from Chi Chi Rodriguez, the famous golfer, at least that's what they told me. Anyway, we squeezed into an old Chevy Impala, and rattled our way into town.

It was Friday night, and there were a lot of people milling around. Carlos was at the wheel and pulled over to the curb. There was a park next to us. Carlos explained that this was the town square and pointed. "Andy, see how the women and men are walking in opposite directions? This is how the men and women meet for the first time.

"You see, if two people feel attracted to each other, they might stop and talk. It is a tradition down here, and they take it seriously. This is where you find nice woman, eh? Next step would be for the man to visit the mother and get her approval before he could court her daughter."

It felt like I was in a time warp. It was hard to believe that these customs still existed, but it was a refreshing change to our liberal ways of meeting the opposite sex. What the hell am I saying, is this the way I want to have it back home? No way!

"I'm hungry, let's go eat." Carlos put the Chevy in gear, and we were off to dinner. He said we were going to the La Concha Shell. "You going to like this place. Chi Chi says this is the best place in town. The seafood is very good, and they have live entertainment, and lots of women."

It was a classy restaurant, and the place was jammed. There was a stage in the dining area, and a bar and dance floor to one side. There was a woman singing, accompanied by a band. A few people were dancing, and there was standing room only at the bar. The maitre d' took us to our table, and the waiter asked if we wanted any drinks. Rum and Coke seemed to be the popular drink, so I ordered the same.

The menu was in Spanish, so Chi Chi translated for me. The food was fantastic and dessert was equally as good. We finished off the meal with coffee and brandy. I was surprised when Carlos ordered the brandy, and the waiter brought a whole bottle to our table. I looked at Carlos, and said, "I know. This is a tradition down here." He laughed, and we all joined in.

The entertainment was traditional-style and was excellent. We were on our second bottle of brandy, and I was getting bombed. I had to take a leak, so I got up and went to the *baños*.

On my way back, I spotted two nice-looking ladies sitting at the bar, so I walked up to them, smiled and introduced myself, and asked the better-looking one to dance. I was pretty wasted but not enough to realize I had made a mistake when she smiled back. Her eyes motioned to say look behind me. I turned and was face to face with a pissed-off Puerto Rican.

"What you think you doing, *gringo*?"

"I asked this lady to dance."

"She my woman."

"I'm sorry, I didn't know that."

I noticed a couple of his friends walk up behind him. *Shit this is great, first night in town, and I'm going to get into a fight.* I started to stiffen up and get prepared to protect myself when I heard Carlos's voice behind me "Hey, Andy, you ready to leave?"

I turned, and saw my guys standing together. I noticed that this dude and his buddies had backed down a little, so I turned to the ladies, bowed, and said I'm sorry. They smiled and accepted my apology, but the guy still had fire in his eyes. Carlos grabbed my shoulder and said, "I think we should get the hell out of here."

When we got outside, they started laughing, and Chi Chi said, "You got a lot of balls *gringo*."

It was getting late, and none of us needed anymore to drink, so we our way back back to the boat, singing and laughing all the way.

I woke up the next morning with a major hangover. I swore I would never drink that brandy again. I washed up, got dressed, and went to the galley to get some coffee.

Red Sky Morning

Most of the crew was having breakfast. They saw me and started chuckling. My dad was amongst them and said, "I hear you had a good time last night."

"Yeah, we had a great time." I left it at that.

Dad said, "You know, I think we should go back to that club tonight"

"You go ahead, because I don't think they'll let me back in there." We all started laughing, and at that point I realized I was now part of the crew. My adventure was moving ahead.

I finished breakfast and went out to get some fresh air. I wasn't feeling very good, and my head was ready to explode. I needed some aspirin, but didn't know where to get some. The captain's quarters were on the top deck next to the bridge, and I was sure that my dad would have some. I climbed up the steps, and went onto the bridge; my dad and the navigator were talking about the new engineer. Frank said he was surprised to find out that the assistant engineer and Ed had worked together before, which could be a good thing. Dad said," I hope so, but I don't know about this guy. He's really a loner, and all he did was drink gin from L.A. to here. Keep an eye on him, Frank."

Dad looked over at me and smiled. "You look like crap. How you feeling?"

"Not so good. You have any aspirins?"

"Come on back to my room, and I'll fix you up."

He not only had aspirin, but some Alka Seltzer. "Thanks, I really needed this."

"These guys like to have a good time, so be careful when you go out with them."

"Don't worry, I will. Hey, Dad, what am I supposed to do during the day? Is there work to do, and who do I report to?"

"Well, right now, there's not much going on, or to do.

You'll report to Carlos when there's work to do, and when we're fishing. The only thing to do right now is keep a tidy ship and wait till we start to unload. The engineer and his assistant will be busy maintaining the engines and generators, which keep our refrigeration system going. By the way, what do you think of the new engineer?"

"I'm not sure, but I think both of them are a little weird and major loners, and Ed drinks too much."

"I agree, so do me a favor and watch them for me. If you see anything funny, let me know."

"Aye-aye, Captain." I saluted and said, "If there's nothing else, sir, I would like permission to go to town to buy a rod and reel and some fishing tackle"

"Get the hell out of here. Oh, by the way, do you need any money?"

"Thanks, I could use a couple of bucks."

He pulled out his wallet and gave me fifty dollars. "Don't spend it all in one place."

I got a cab to town, figuring if there wasn't much to do on the boat, I'd buy some fishing gear and try my luck around the waterfront. I went all over town looking for a sporting goods store. I was just about ready to give up when I spotted a store across the street. I was all excited until I saw what they had to offer. A salesman asked if he could help me, and I explained what I was looking for. "He said I wouldn't find anything in town, but there was a tackle shop at the marina that had the equipment I was looking for.

Shit, I had wasted a whole day in town, because the marina was walking distance from the boat. Oh well, I now knew where to get my gear, so I decided to kill a little more time, scope out the sights, then get back to the boat for lunch.

When I got back to the boat, I went straight to the galley, where most of the crew was starting to sit down for lunch. There was a major conversation going on about someone that got injured while unloading fish that morning. Apparently, they finished unloading one well and were unbolting the hatch to the next well. All the bolts were off, but the hatch was stuck. Unexpectedly, the hatch and the tuna coming out behind it blew open and crushed one guy. He was seriously injured and was transported to a bigger hospital in San Juan.

 I knew how difficult and dangerous it was to unload fish, because my friends and I would hire out to unload fish at the canneries in San Pedro. Our fathers or relatives ran the boats, and there were always a few of the crew who would rather spend time with their families instead of unloading fish for three or four days. They paid well for us to replace them.

 Fishing boats like the *Western Ace* had two main fish wells with open access from the deck and above. The hatch openings are approximately ten feet square, making them large enough to unload the tuna with a crane and a large bucket lowered into the well. The two main wells held about forty to fifty tons of tuna each, and the balance of the wells held from twenty to forty tons each, based on their location in the hull.

 The balance of the wells had small hatches deck-side for loading fish, and at the bottom of a well there was a door-sized hatch that led from one well to another to the main wells.

 Prior to unloading the tuna, the engineer would start raising the temperature of the brine water to start thawing out the tuna. When we finished unloading the main hatch, we would have to remove the door-sized hatch to the next well. This was extremely dangerous, because the next well had thirty tons of fish in it, and if thawed out properly the tuna would come pouring out as soon as the hatch was removed. Sometimes the force of the tuna would cause the hatch door, which weighed a couple of hundred pounds to go flying across the empty well. I'm sure that was what happened to that man who was injured.

This method of unloading fish was rated as the most physical and dangerous job. Each tuna could range from five to over two hundred and fifty pounds. It's extremely cold, dirty, slimy, wet, and slippery, with no level footing. Many times the tuna are not totally thawed, and we had to use crowbars to break each fish loose. I remember hurting all over after one day of unloading, and after three days, I was totally exhausted, and I'm young and in great physical shape. The only good thing was, I'd make a couple of hundred bucks.

As lunch progressed the conversation changed. The main topic was how anxious everybody was to get unloaded and go fishing, which is understandable because the crew didn't make any money sitting in port. Their income was based on their share of the net profit of the fish caught.

Talking about catching fish reminded me that I'd just bought some fishing gear, and it was time to try it out. Chi Chi told me that the fishing was pretty good at the end of the pier where we were tied up. He wanted to come along, so I grabbed my gear, and we took off. It was about a quarter of a mile walk from the boat, and there were a couple of guys fishing there. Chi Chi had a little talk with one of them, and said, "Fishing is a little slow right now, but the tide is coming in and it should get better in a couple of hours."

They were catching, what they called Redfish. Chi Chi said they were really good to eat, and if I caught any, we could bring them back to John. We asked the fisherman what they were using for bait. They were using live shrimp, and one of them had more than he needed, so I bought some off of him for a dollar.

These guys knew what they were talking about, because an hour and a half went by before anyone caught anything. One of the guys pulled in a nice-sized Redfish that was at least five pounds. That got my attention, and a minute later I got a bite. I set the hook and was surprised at the fight it put up. This one was a little bigger, maybe six to seven pounds.

In forty-five minutes, I had landed three nice Redfish. Chi Chi told me he had never fished with a rod and reel, but only a hand line or a net. I handed him the rod and said, "Hey, *amigo*, its time you tried."

"*Muchas gracias.*"

He went crazy when he hooked a fish, and when he got it in he started jumping around just like a kid. The fishermen were cracking up. He grabbed that Redfish, pretended to kiss it, put it in our bucket, and couldn't get bait back in the water fast enough. I was having a ball watching Chi Chi fish. He caught three more, and I said, "Don't you think we have enough fish?"

He gave me a sad look and said, "Come on, let me catch some more." He gave me a big smile "OK *gringo*, let's take these fish to John, he's going to love them."

By the time we got back to the boat, it was dinnertime, and some of the crew was already in the galley. Chi Chi was prancing around the deck with the bucket of fish, bragging about how he had caught them. Carlos made us a drink, and we celebrated our catch. John was excited and said he would make something special for lunch the next day.

You know, I was really starting to have a good time and felt lucky that I made this trip.

Chapter 6

There was little work to do on the boat, and for the next few days I fished, went to the beach, where I found a good body surfing spot, and at night, I went out with the guys. I helped John cook and clean up the galley. We prepared fresh Redfish three or four different ways, and I knew I better find some other fish to catch. I walked over to the marina and talked to some of the fisherman. There were no charter or party boats available, but I met a really cool guy that owned a twenty-four foot fishing boat. Armando was a local businessman, and his family owned a couple of restaurants in town. He went fishing every other day and took his catch to the restaurants. He asked me if I would like to go fishing with him, and of course I accepted. We planned to meet at the marina a 6:00 the next morning and spend the whole day fishing.

I got to the marina at 5:45, and Armando was already on his boat with the engine running. He spotted me. "Good, you're early. Let's go catch some bait before we go fishing." I untied the mooring lines, Armando backed out the boat, and we were off. He stopped at the harbor entrance where we dropped a couple of hand lines over the side. Each line had three or four small feather jigs tied to it, and we would jerk them up and down to attract the bait. Armando knew what he was doing, and in twenty minutes, we had a full bait tank of small mackerel.

The weather was beautiful, and Armando decided to troll a couple of marlin jigs. I had caught a lot of different fish in my life, but never a marlin. We were trolling for over an hour when Armando said, "Andy, look over there. A marlin tail fin."

I not only saw one, but three or four fins moving through the water. Armando turned the boat towards them and made a circle around the area. I saw a marlin following the jig, and a second later he attacked it. Armando pushed the throttle forward to set the hook. He told me to grab the rod as he started reeling in the other line. It happened so quickly and there I was, fighting a big-ass marlin. It was jumping and shaking its head, trying to lose the hook, but I kept a taut line and fought him every second.

Armando yelled, "You doing really good. It's a big fish, maybe three hundred pounds!"

It took close to an hour to get the marlin to the side of the boat. Armando gaffed it, and I helped him get it on the swim step. We tied it down, made sure it was secure, and got back to catching fish. I was so pumped up. I couldn't believe how lucky I was. In ten minutes we were on another fish. This time it was a big dorado. Armando reeled it in, and I gaffed it. Armando said, "Looks like a big school of fish. Let's try bait." We both cast baits in the water and were hooked up instantly.

By lunchtime we had a full deck of fish. We caught dorado, wahoo, rock cod, a couple of huge groupers, and don't forget my marlin.

Armando asked, "You had enough for the day?"

I said, "It's up to you. Do we have enough fish for your restaurant?"

"Are you kidding? This is way too much for me. Maybe your crew would like some fresh fish. We'll stop by your boat and drop some off, and you can show them your marlin."

This guy was really cool and I couldn't wait to show off our catch.

We tied up to the *Western Ace*. Everybody, including my dad, checked out the marlin. Armando said he was going to smoke some of the marlin and would drop some off. We unloaded some dorado, a couple of wahoo, and one grouper. John was really appreciative, thanking Armando over and over. He invited Armando to join us for lunch and he accepted. We had a traditional Croatian meal of mostaccioli, roast beef, and sauerkraut. We talked about our fishing trip. You'd think that the crew would care less about fishing, but none of them except Chi Chi had ever caught a fish on a rod and reel, and Armando was having a great time telling them about it. Before he left, Armando invited all of us to come for dinner, at his restaurant.

I was watching Armando's boat heading toward the marina when my dad leaned on the rail next to me. "He's a hell of a nice guy. You were lucky to meet someone like that."

"Yeah, I know. I told him we would be here for a couple more weeks, and he invited me to go fishing with him any time I wanted. By the way, how are things going at the cannery?"

"I told them that we're on a tight schedule and want to travel up the East Coast with the rest of the fleet. They said they're doing everything possible to expedite the process. They'll finish unloading the *Chicken of the Sea* today. The next boat in line is not part of our group and only holds four hundred tons. They're going to start unloading this afternoon and work through the weekend. If everything goes well, they'll start unloading our sister ship, the *Western King* on Monday. That leaves the *Pioneer,* which is anchored in the bay. It holds a thousand tons and will take at least four days to unload. I don't know too much about them, because the boat's port is Panama, but I did meet the skipper this morning. What an asshole. All he did was brag about his boat and crew, then bitched like hell about the delay. Well, I have to go back to the cannery for another meeting, so I'll see you for dinner."

By six, most of the crew was ready to go. We had two cabs and Chi Chi's Chevy to transport us to Armando's. We got to his restaurant around six-thirty. My new friend greeted us at the door, "Welcome to Armando's. Follow me, your table is ready."

It was a classy restaurant and pretty crowded for a Thursday evening. Armando insisted that he order our dinner. He introduced our waiters, told them to take our drink orders, and to keep them flowing. We were having a great time. The food was fantastic and just kept coming. It seemed that each course was better than the last. When we finished dinner, the waiters brought coffee, espresso, after-dinner drinks, and some sumptuous desserts to choose from. Armando pulled up a chair and joined us. My dad turned to Armando and said, "This was a fantastic meal, and the service is as good as it gets. Let me take care of the bill."

"No way, it is my pleasure to pick up the tab. I had a wonderful time with your son, and you invited me for lunch, which I really enjoyed. If you like, you can take care of the waiters; I'm sure they would appreciate it. Excuse me for a moment. I'll be right back."

Dad looked at me and said, "Now that's a real gentleman."

Armando came back to our table with a box of Cuban

cigars. "*Senores*, please help yourselves." Most of us smoked cigarettes, and my dad smoked cigars, but all of us lit up a Havana. I took a puff, and said, "A perfect way to finish a great meal."

Dad held out the cigar and said, "These are delicious; I have to ask Armando where I can get a few boxes before we leave Puerto Rico."

It's unfortunate, but someone has to be on watch twenty-four hours a day on the boat. It was the assistant engineer's turn tonight, and when we got back, he was on the deck waiting for us. "You won't believe what's happening on the *Pionee*r. There's a wild party going on, and there's a bunch of naked women running around the deck."

We all ran over to the portside to see what was going on. It was wild all right. The music was echoing through the harbor, people were yelling and screaming, and yes, there were some nude woman running around the deck. We passed the binoculars around so we could get a closer look. Some of the crew and the women were skinny-dipping and jumping off the side of the boat. Others were dancing and being rowdy.

Carlos said, "Well, this tops off the night. I've seen enough, I'm going to bed."

Most of us did the same, but it was impossible to sleep with all that noise. It was around two in the morning when things started to settle down, and it didn't take long before we were all snoring away.

It was a religious custom, not to eat meat on Friday. John was preparing tuna spaghetti for lunch, which sounded good. My dad was at another meeting, which lasted all morning, and just got back in time for lunch.

Dad stood up and said, "We have a couple of guests for lunch: Frank Pagano, captain of the *Western King,* and the navigator, Larry Peterson. I've also got some great news.

The party on the *Pioneer* last night got out of hand. Some of the hookers they had on the boat got beat up a little and complained to the police. The local Coast Guard boarded the boat this morning and found one girl under age and another pretty messed up. They checked the boat's papers and licenses, and found some problems. It was decided that until the skipper cleared these up, they would not be allowed to unload. Which means we go before them. That will save us four to five days, which means we will be no more than a day behind the fleet."

The news got everybody excited, because if there is no fish, there's no money.

It was 5:00 A.M. Sunday morning, and I was at the marina to go fishing with Armando.

"Good morning Andy. Ready to go"?

"Absolutely. I'll get the lines".

We were catching bait when I asked, "So where are we fishing today? Going after any marlin"?

"No, I think we're going to stay close to shore, because I'm worried about the weather."

"It looks beautiful to me".

"There is an old saying: Red sky at night, sailor's delight, Red sky morning, sailor's warning. As you can see, the sunrise is very red, and you see those big clouds on the horizon? They could bring some rain and shitty weather."

"I've heard of that saying before. I guess it's better not to mess around with Mother Nature.

So, what's the plan?"

"I think we'll run up the coast about fifteen miles and fish for bass and snapper."

About thirty minutes went by before Armando started to slow down. "How do you know where to fish?" I asked.

He explained that he used landmarks. "See that point to your right and that big rock to your left. I try to make a tri-

Red Sky Morning

angle, using the boat as the third mark."

"When I think about it, we sort of use the same methods back in California."

He certainly knew the spot, because in only a couple of minutes, I got a bite. I pulled in a nice red snapper, weighing about six or seven pounds. Armando hooked up but on something a lot bigger. He said, "Get the gaff." Five minutes later, I gaffed a forty-pound grouper and lifted it over the side. About an hour went by, and the fish box was over half-full. "Pretty good fishing, huh," said Armando.

"I can't believe it; we must have caught over two hundred pounds of fish."

"I normally do pretty good here, but today it's been exceptional. Maybe we should think about going in soon. Those big clouds we saw this morning are getting closer, and I think we're in for some bad weather."

I turned on the electric winch and started to pull up the anchor. When I had all the slack pulled in, the winch came to a halt. "Hey, Armando, I think the anchor is stuck."

"Shit, that's all we need"

We tried everything, moving the boat forward and backward. Almost an hour went by, and we still had no success. It started raining, and the wind was picking up. I could tell that Armando was getting worried.

"I'm going to try one more time. If the anchor doesn't break loose, we'll cut the chain and get the hell out of here."

He put it in reverse and pushed the throttle all the way. It didn't budge. He turned out to sea and punched it. When the chain came tight, the shock almost knocked me overboard. I was hanging onto the rail and realized that we were moving. I yelled to Armando, "I think we broke free!"

"Get on the winch and pull up that anchor. We need to get going."

It was starting to blow pretty hard by the time we

started back. The waves were hitting us broadside, so we couldn't go very fast. It was around five miles to the point Armando used as a landmark. When we rounded the point, the ocean was even worse. It started to get a little scary, especially when the swells became a lot bigger bigger than the boat.

We had to really slow down, and when a bigger swell got close, Armando would have to turn into it or we could capsize. "I can't believe how fast this storm hit. It's going to be tough to get back to the harbor, but don't worry; this is a good, seaworthy boat."

"I'm happy to hear that. Look at size of that swell."

Armando was already reacting, turning the bow to face it. He pushed the throttle forward, and the wave broke over us. When we got past that wave, Armando yelled, "I don't think we can make it back to Ponce!"

"What are we going to do?"

"There's a small fishing village a couple of miles from here, and they have a breakwater that protects the marina. If we can get in there, we'll be safe."

Armando maneuvered the boat the best he could, and we slowly made headway. Twenty minutes later, he turned toward the shore, putting the waves at our stern. It was a little hairy. As the wave pushed us we sped up and surfed the crest of the wave until it passed us. Then we fell into the trough of the next wave, and back up on the crest. Armando was doing a great job keeping us from being swamped.

Armando pointed toward shore. "Can you see the breakwater?" I could see it and some buildings behind it. "Don't worry, we're going to make it."

Make it! Shit! I didn't think there was a chance that we wouldn't. Now, I was really scared.

As we neared the opening of the jetty, I could see that

Red Sky Morning

the waves was breaking over the rock barrier and through the opening. "We're going to have to ride those waves in," Armando said.

"They're over ten feet. Do you think we can make it?"

"We have no choice. We stay out here, and the waves might swamp us."

"The same thing could happen surfing those waves in."

"If that happens, we can swim to shore. Out in the open ocean, we would probably drown."

"What do you want me to do?"

"Just hang on. Here we go."

Armando steered his boat to the right side of the opening. The direction of the waves were from right to left, so if we caught the wave properly we'd surf the break to the left. I could see the fear in Armando's eyes as the wave built behind us. It was at least ten feet and starting to break. Armando's timing was perfect, and he pushed the throttle to full as we shot down the face of the wave. I couldn't believe we were riding this wave in a twenty-four foot boat!

Time seemed to stand still, and everything was in slow motion. I looked at Armando. He looked at me and smiled, then let out a yell,"Yeehah! Were going to make it."

We rode the wave across the opening, and when we reached the left side We were inside the relative calm and safety of the breakwater. We both started yelling and jumping up and down.

"I can't believe we made it," said Armando.

"Yeah, that was a real white-knuckler."

As soon as we cleared the breakwater, it was fairly calm, and Armando headed for the dock. We tied down the boat, made sure everything was secure and headed for town. It was pouring, and I estimated the winds were gusting from thirty to forty miles an hour.

"So, what are we going to do now?" I asked.

"The first thing is to contact my family and your father, because we'll be stuck here tonight. Next, we find a motel, if there is one."

There was a restaurant/bar across the street from the marina. We went inside. There were a few guys and a couple of women at the bar. "Is there a phone I can use?" Armando asked.

"Sure, you can use mine," said the bartender.

Armando tried calling his home and both of his restaurants but couldn't get through. He called the operator, who said the lines were down due to an accident where a truck hit a telephone pole. She expected it to be repaired sometime the next day. Armando shook his head. "Jesus Christ, what the hell am I going to do?"

I don't know how I thought of it, but a possible solution popped into my head. "Armando, if we can find someone with a marine radio, we could call the *Western Ace*."

"What a great idea."

Armando asked the bartender, "Does anybody here own a boat with a marine radio on it."

"I've got one on my boat. My name is Andres. Give me a couple of minutes, and I'll go down to the marina with you."

We ran down to Andres's boat, and Armando made the call.

"*Western Ace*, this is the *Armando II* calling." He tried over and over, with no response.

"Try the *Western King*, maybe someone is in their pilothouse".

He made the call and waited. "This is Frank Pagano, captain of the *Western King*. What can I do for you?" Armando handed me the mike.

"This is Andy Rafkin. My father is the captain of the *Western Ace*."

"Your dad just left my boat; he was starting to worry about you. This little squall ended up to be a pretty big storm."

"Please tell him we're OK, and that we pulled into Pelican Bay to get away from the storm. We plan to spend the night here and head back to Ponce as soon as the weather blows over."

"Your dad was going back to the *Ace*. I'll go over there right now. It'll take me ten minutes to get there. Please stand by, and I'll have him call you"

* * *

"*Armando II*, this is the *Western Ace* calling"

"This is the *Armando II*. Hi, Dad."

"I'm glad to hear that everything is OK. Where's Pelican Bay?"

"It's about ten miles up the coast. We were on our way back to Ponce when Armando decided that we better head for cover."

"That was a wise thing to do. I checked on the weather and it should clear by tomorrow morning. Frank told me you're going to spend the night there. Does Armando need me to do anything for him?"

I handed the mike to Armando, who explained that the local phones were dead. He gave my dad some phone numbers to call. "This is the *Armando II*. Thank you, and we'll see you *mañana*."

"This is the *Western Ace,* over and out."

Armando asked, "Hey Andres, where's a good place to stay tonight?"

"There are two motels in town. I think the smaller one is better. Let's go back to my bar, and I'll buy you two a drink"

One drink led to another while we told Andres about our adventure. Armando said, "I don't know about you, but I'm ready to find that motel, check in, and get some dinner." We thanked Andres for his hospitality and went looking for the motel.

It was more like a boarding house. The innkeeper checked us in and recommended a place to eat about a block away. He said the food was very good, and they had a bar. We had no luggage, so we walked directly to the restaurant. About half way through my first drink, I realized how tired I was.

"Man, am I pooped. This has been a long day," Armando said.

We didn't talk much more, but we pounded down a few more drinks and wolfed down our dinner. Armando picked up the tab, we went back to the motel, and straight to our rooms. I took a hot shower and went out like a light.

Chapter 7

We were back at the Ponce marina by ten in the morning. The fish we caught the previous day were covered with ice and still in good shape. I helped Armando get the fish into his truck, and he dropped me off at the *Ace*. We planned to go fishing again Wednesday, weather permitting.

I was headed for the bunkroom when I ran into my dad. "Glad to see you back. Everything OK?"

"Yeah, a shower and a change of clothes, and I'll be fine."

"I'm going to the *Western King* for lunch. You want to join me?"

"Sounds good to me. When are you going?"

"Why don't you meet me in my cabin in an hour."

When we arrived on the *King,* they were still unloading fish. The Captain, Frank Pagano, came over to greet us, "You've got to see this guy we hired to unload fish. I've never seen anybody so fast in my life."

We walked over to the hatch, and Frank pointed him out. They were unloading skipjack tuna that weighed four to six pounds. This guy had a steady flow of two or three fish flying through the air and into the bucket. "He's been going at that rate since we started this morning"

My dad said, "Be sure to tell him that I'll hire him when he's finished here. By the way, I spoke to Nick Trutanich, and he said he and his partners are flying down here Thursday morning. He said that he spoke to StarKist about starting to unload the *Ace* before you're finished, and they agreed to start Wednesday morning."

"That's great. We better plan to take them to a nice place Thursday night. You know how they like to be wined and dined."

"I'll make reservations at the Hotel Del Rey. It's a nice place, and has an excellent restaurant and entertainment"

Lunch was OK, but John was definitely the better cook. When we got back to the *Ace,* John greeted us in Croatian, "Armando stopped by and dropped off some smoked marlin, maybe thirty or forty pounds. We'll have smoked fish for the whole trip."

That reminded me to call Armando to let him know I couldn't go fishing with him Wednesday, because I would be unloading fish.

The captain went to his cabin, and I headed for the bunkroom, where I ran into Carlos. "Hey, Andy, I been looking for you"

"What's happening?"

"I wanted to know if you would like to go out with us tonight."

"Sure, where we going?"

"That's a surprise. Be ready at six."

The Chevy was running, and Chi Chi yelled, "*Vamonos*. We waiting for you."

I jumped into the car, and Chi Chi took off. "Were not going to La Concha?" They all laughed.

Carlos said, "We going someplace very special."

Red Sky Morning

"*Si*, lots of *señoritas.* Yee ha!"

We definitely weren't headed to town, because the road climbed into the foothills, in fact, I could see the town lights below. About fifteen minutes later, Chi Chi pulled up to a gated entrance. There was a speaker, and he introduced himself. The gate opened, and we drove down to a big villa.

"Come on *gringo*, let's go"

We walked into the main courtyard and through the front door. Music was playing, and there were a lot of good-looking women around, but no guys.

"This is your surprise," said Carlos. "You pick one of these beautiful women, and she is yours for the night. The rest of us will find our own. We already pay for you, so have some fun."

I had a feeling I knew what kind of place this was, and Carlos confirmed it. I had never been with a prostitute, but there's always a first time. I walked around and scoped out the girls. Most of them were young, maybe sixteen to early twenties. Some of them looked a little rough around the edges, and I was sure that they'd had a hard life.

Chi Chi came by and said, "Have fun." He handed me a beer, then he turned and put his arm around a cute *señorita* and walked off. I was now the only male left in the room, and I was getting a little nervous. I walked out to the courtyard, and found her sitting next to a fountain. She spoke a little English, and my Spanish had improved since I got to Puerto Rico, so we sat and talked for awhile. She was very exotic-looking, with beautiful big dark eyes and long jet-black hair. We seemed to get along. Of course, that was part of her job wasn't it?

Her name was Rosa, and she asked if I wanted something to eat. I accepted. She took me by the arm and escorted me to the dining room. We drank, ate, and were having some genuine fun. I asked her to dance, and we whirled around the dance floor. Then the music slowed down, and I pulled her close. *God, if I got any closer, I'd be behind her.* She had a great body, and I could feel all her assets pushing against me. She turned her face to mine and kissed me gently on the lips. She whispered in my ear, "Would you like to go to my room?"

"I'd love to."

She guided me toward the stairs, and I was a little uncomfortable, because I had the biggest hard-on, I tried to conceal it, but there was no way.

I was sexually active back home, and I thought I was a studly kind of guy at sixteen, but this nineteen-year-old showed me things I didn't know existed. Every time I thought I couldn't do it again, Rosa had ways to keep me going and going. Two hours went by, and I was totally spent. I lay back and lit a cigarette while Rosa rested her head on my chest. I was stroking her hair, and she whispered, "You must believe me. I don't normally give a man this much pleasure, but tonight, I had a wonderful time. You made me feel so special, and you really make me feel so good in bed. I just want more of you."

She giggled and kissed my chest, than slowly kissed a path toward my groin. I thought there was no way, but Rosa possessed some kind of magic, and I found myself again wrapped in her arms, both of us moaning and groaning and wanting more.

I felt someone lightly shaking me. I opened my eyes and saw Rosa smiling. "I let you sleep for a while. Now it's getting late, and you have to go. Your friends are waiting for you downstairs."

I knew Rosa was a hooker, but I would never forget this evening. I went to her and gave her, hugged and kissed her, and said, "Thank you for a wonderful evening." Her eyes welled up with little tears when she smiled. I turned and shut the door.

We were winding down the hilly road when Carlos said, "She must have been very good, because we waited almost two hours for you."

I rested my head back on the seat and said, "Thank you, guys, for taking me tonight. I really had a good time." I shut my eyes. *If they only knew; then, maybe they did.*

The sunlight shone through my porthole, and woke me up. It was 6:00 A.M., but I definitely wasn't ready to get up. I really didn't have anything to do that morning, so I rolled over and tried to get a couple more of hours of shut-eye. I woke up around 7:30 and lay in bed for another half-hour. I was daydreaming about the previous evening when Carlos came to my bunk.

"Hey, Andy, time to get up."

"What's going on?"

"We need to get ready for unloading fish tomorrow."

"OK, I'll be right out." But first, I thought, I better quit thinking of Rosa and let this hard-on calm down before I jump out of bed.

I got dressed and went to the galley for a cup of coffee. I heard the main engines start, so I went out on deck and saw a couple of our guys untying the lines. I asked Carlos what was going on. He said we were moving up to where the cannery cranes were, so they could unload us tomorrow. They had big buckets, about four feet high and six feet in diameter. The crane lowered the buckets into the hatch. The buckets held approximately five to six hundred pounds of fish and when fully loaded, would be lifted dockside and transported to the cannery for weighing and processing.

After lunch, we removed the two main hatch covers to check on the condition of the tuna. The fish had been slowly thawing for some time, in anticipation of unloading them, and were in perfect shape for starting the following day. The rest of the day flew by, we finished dinner, and I went up to the bridge to have a smoke. My dad came out of his cabin with an unlit cigar in his mouth. He lit the cigar and said, "I heard you had a really good time the other night."

"Couldn't get much better. You know, these guys have treated me like one of their own, and I've had a ton of fun with them."

"Glad to hear you're enjoying yourself."

"You know, Dad, I'm really looking forward to the trip."

"Well, you'll start working tomorrow, and as soon as we finish unloading, I plan to leave immediately. By the way, the owners will be here tomorrow, and we're going out for the evening. I thought you might like to go."

"Count me in, Captain".

The next morning, I was up and ready to go to work. I took inventory of the gear I would wear, when I was unloading fish. Rubber boots, rain slicks, hardhat, rubber gloves, hand-held ice hook were all there. I laid them out on the bunk and went to the galley for a big hearty breakfast. Unloading fish was a tough job, and I'd need the extra fuel to burn.

We took the hatches off the two main wells. Each well held forty tons of tuna, and five of us would be in each well. At 7:30 sharp, the first buckets were lowered to the deck. If the tuna were small, five to fifteen pounds, we would grab them by the tails, and flip them into the bucket. The tuna we started unloading weighed between twenty and forty pounds, so we used the ice hook in one hand to hook the mouth, grab the tail with the other, and lift and throw it into the bucket. Try doing this all day as fast as you can. I guarantee you won't want to come back the next day.

Red Sky Morning

By midafternoon, we finished unloading the first well. Now came the dangerous part of unbolting the lower hatch connecting to the next well.

There are ten bolts holding the hatch, and you slowly loosen them. There are twenty to thirty-five tons of fish pushing against that hatch, and when the bolts are undone the tuna can burst like an icy avalanche through the hatch with so much force, a man could get crushed.

This time, however, the hatch had little pressure against it. When we removed the hatch we found out why. First, the tuna were huge, about 200-300 pounds, and they were not totally thawed out which meant using crowbars and sledge hammers to loosen them. This is a hard and slow process, but the only way. The tuna were too big to lift into the buckets, so we tied a rope to its tail, and the crane pulled up two or three at a time. I can't tell you how exhausting this was.

We stopped at six, climbed into the bucket, and the crane lifted us to the deck. We washed and scrubbed down our gear, then hung it up to dry. I couldn't wait to take a hot shower, which felt fantastic. I've done this before, and knew I'd be hurting later.

When we sat down for dinner, my hands were so sore that I could barely hold a fork, but I was starving and managed to fill my plate a couple of times. I poured myself another glass of red wine and went out on deck to have a smoke. I leaned on the rail and watched the sunset.

"Just a few more days, and we'll be heading for the East Coast. I can't wait."

I recognized the voice and turned. "Hey, Frank, you must be getting tired of this place. As for me, except for today, I've been having a great time."

"I've heard about your adventures."

"You know, that's a good way to describe my last two

weeks, but I agree its time to get out of here."

"Well, Andy, it's been a long day, and I'm going to hit the sack. I'll see you in the mourning."

"I'll be right behind you. Goodnight".

When I woke up my whole body ached. I stretched out the best I could and went to work. The day flew by. I finished cleaning my gear and got ready to go out with my dad and the owners of the boat.

We were to meet in the galley, and I was the first one there. Dad and Frank were next, and the owners followed them in. Introductions were made, then we walked down the ramp to a Ford van the owners had rented. We stopped at the StarKist office and picked up the general manager, Tony Casara. It took about twenty minutes to get to the Hotel and Resort, a real classy place. The grounds were beautiful. We checked in at the restaurant and followed the maitre d' to our table. The band was playing bossa nova type music, and there were a few couples out on the dance floor.

We ordered cocktails and started to review our menus. The main topic of conversation was our next trip. Three of the boats were already in the fishing area, and the *Chicken of the Sea* and the *Western King* would be leaving as soon as the *King* finished unloading.

"Andy, when do you think you'll be ready to go?" asked Mr.Trutanich.

"I hired a couple more guys to help unload. They started this morning, and our production has really increased. If we don't run into any major problems, we should be finished Saturday. We're already taking on provisions, and I made arrangements to fuel up Saturday evening."

"So, you think you'll pull out of here Sunday?"

"Again, if all goes well, I plan to set sail early Sunday morning".

We finished dinner, and I started checking out the local

action. This place was a lot more sophisticated than the smaller clubs, and I knew that I might have to ask a mother if I could dance with her daughter.

I had to take a pee, so I excused myself and went looking for the *baños*. Before I went back to our table, I looked around. Most of the tables held couples or business people, and I spotted a few single women, but they were too young or not too pretty. As I neared our table, I spotted a beauty walking by. She sat down with an older couple that were probably her parents. The music stopped and I thought it was the opportune time to ask her to dance. I walked over to her table, smiled at her, and sort of asked her and her mother together if she would like to dance. She turned to her mother, who nodded.

She stood up, and I offered her my hand. We reached the dance floor at the same time the band started playing a slow sort of samba. As we danced, I introduced myself, and she did the same. She was truly a fox, and I thought, man, I wish I could have met her under different circumstances. She seemed a little nervous, and I, the big butt-man couldn't even start a conversation.

I finally blurted out, "It's *mucha coolo* here, than at my casa." Her eyes widened, and then she looked very pissed off. She pushed away from me and slapped me across the face. She turned away and stomped back to her table leaving, me on the dance floor, with a lot of eyes staring at me. What the hell had I done to get her so upset? She was talking to her mother, and both of them were giving me an ugly glare. I decided to get to my table and hide.

"What the hell happened out there?" asked my dad.

"I don't know. I didn't do anything. In fact, we barely spoke. All I said was, it's *mucha cooler* here, and than she slapped me." The general manager of StarKist said there must have been some kind of misunderstanding. He went over and sat down with them. They were talking away, and after a few minutes, they all started laughing. Now, I was really confused.

Tony came back to our table, cracking up. "You know what she thought you said"?

"What?"

"She thought you said, *mucho culo*. You know, like, much ass, or lots of ass, and then you said something about your *casa*. Basically, she thought you were propositioning her to go with you to your *casa*. You bad boy." Everybody started laughing and I joined in, but I still felt embarrassed.

I felt I had to apologize, but everybody thought I should leave it alone. I couldn't, so I walked over to their table, bowed my head, and said I was sorry for the misunderstanding. They started laughing, and she looked up at me and smiled. I thought, all right, I'd ask her to dance again. Her mother must have been reading my mind, and the look she gave me said, not on your life, buddy. I smiled, and wished them goodnight. Walking back, I thought, Puerto Rico was great, but I couldn't wait to get back to the States get started fishing for tuna and make some money.

Chapter 8

It was around one in the morning when I woke up with that urge to relieve myself. Coming back to my bunk, I tried to prepare myself to relax and get back to sleep. As I lay there, thoughts of my adventure crept into my consciousness. At first, I fought it and tried to clear my head. I shut my eyes and started to daydream.

A little more than two weeks had gone by since I left San Pedro, and my life had been jam-packed with action. The first day and my first time on a plane, I thought I was going crash and die. I visualized the stewardess falling, the passengers screaming, the sight of the plane's wings flapping in the turbulence, and my dad telling me how worried he was. Wow!

Getting to Ponce, meeting the crew, meeting Armando, and catching my first marlin, then going to town with the guys, —things couldn't be much better. Then Armando and I getting caught in that storm, meeting Rosa, and the fantastic night we spent together, that was awesome. Wow, I realized I was getting a woody. *Man, I'd like to see her again.* As I cleared my mind of Rosa, I saw myself standing on the dance floor holding my cheek, —*mucho coolo*— I'll be careful not to say that again. I chuckled at the thought, and lay there thinking how lucky I was. A few minutes later I dozed off.

It was still dark when I woke up. We planned to leave Ponce at 5:30, so I decided to stay in my bunk a little longer. I wondered where the next part of my adventure would take me, who I would meet, what the fishing would be like.

I was glad I had enough time to say goodbye to Armando. Meeting him was the best thing that had happened so far. We promised to stay in touch, but deep down, I knew he would only become a good memory. I looked at my watch; it was quarter to five, so I decided to get up and get down to the galley.

"Hey, John, good morning. What's for breakfast?"

"*Dobra Utrough*," which meant good morning in Croatian. "I'm not cooking this morning, only toast and sweet rolls. Were pulling out soon, and everybody's going to be busy. Want some coffee?"

"Sure, I hope it's nice and strong." John poured me a cup, and I picked out a gooey-looking sweet roll and headed out on the deck. Most of the crew was milling around, moving this or securing that.

"*Buenos dias*, Carlos. You have anything for me to do?"

"Good morning, Andy. Everything's ready to go, so you might as well take it easy."

I pulled out my pack of Marlboros and offered Carlos one. He used his lighter to light mine then his. "I hope you had a nice time in Ponce."

"Carlos, I can't thank you enough for being so nice."

"We had some good fun together, eh?"

"If it wasn't for you and Chi Chi, it would have been

Red Sky Morning

pretty boring. Again, thanks for everything. You guys really helped make my stay in Ponce an adventure I won't forget."

"It was fun for me too. By the way the captain was looking for you; I think he's on the bridge."

I left Carlos on deck, and went up to the bridge. I found my dad and Frank looking over some navigational charts. "Plotting our course?"

"Good morning, son. That's exactly what we're doing, come here and I'll show you. See here, Ponce is on the south side of Puerto Rico, in the Caribbean Sea. When we leave Ponce, we'll head west, then go north around Puerto Rico's west coast, and enter the Atlantic here. Then we set our course northwest and head up the East Coast."

"Will we go by any islands in the Bahamas?"

"We'll get fairly close to the most southern island of the Bahamas, but we'll probably be too far away to see anything."

"When do we start looking for fish?"

"When we start up the Florida coast. We probably won't find any fish until we're farther north, but we'll be keeping a sharp look out."

The skipper pulled out a Cuban, lit it up, and said, "I'm glad Armando turned me onto these. They're excellent, so I stocked up on them. Don't want to run out during this trip, and I'd hate to go back to what I used to smoke."

"So what's our first port of call?"

"Well, our target area to fish is off the coasts of Delaware to Maine, so we plan to pull into port near Baltimore, Maryland, to take on fuel and whatever else we need. We're about 1300 miles from there, which will take us almost five days, if the weather remains stable. So did you have fun in Ponce?"

"Yeah, it's been a blast."

"You seemed to get along with the crew?"

"With most of them. We had some really good times in Ponce, and I feel like I've made some good friends."

"You know, I was pretty busy in Ponce, and I didn't notice how things were going. How about the new engineer, Ed, and his assistant, Jack? What does the crew think of them?"

"I think I can speak for the whole crew. Ed's an asshole, and Jack follows everything Ed does, and acts just like him."

"Does Ed drink a lot?"

"Definitely, and so does his sidekick. I've seen him drinking, drunk, or passed out at night, and I've seen him a little buzzed during the day. Just yesterday at lunch he was feeling no pain, and he got really obnoxious. He started cussing at John about the type of food he served, calling it 'European ethnic shit,' and then started to criticize his meals, calling him a crappy cook.

"That really got the crew pissed off, and pretty much in unison, they told him to get the fuck out of the galley. Ed dumped his plate on the table and said he didn't know how all of us could eat this shit, then staggered out with his buddy, Jack. Carlos and John jumped to their feet, and started after Ed. I'm sure if Chi Chi hadn't stopped them, they would have kicked the shit out of those assholes."

Dad took a big puff of his Havana and blew out a plume of smoke. "Well, son, that confirms the sort of the stuff I'm hearing. Not only is he a drunk and a bad influence on Jack, but he fucked up big time, setting some of the instruments and valves that control the refrigeration system during the time we were unloading. Fortunately, before Frank left Thursday morning, he made his normal rounds and spotted the incorrect settings. If he hadn't found them about a third of the wells would have frozen solid, and we would have been delayed by two or three days. I'm not sure what to do with them. I didn't hire him, so I'm going to radio the owners and try to find a solution."

We talked for a while about fishing and navigation, then I left the skipper and his mate hovering over some charts, and went to the galley to see what was for lunch. When I entered the kitchen, John was pulling some packages out of the freezer. "Hey, John, how's it going?"

"I get some chicken out for lunch early so it can defrost."

"How you going to prepare it?"

"Carlos and I decided to have a barbecue today. Sounds good huh?"

"Everybody loves barbecue chicken. Can I help cook?"

"Sure, come back about noon and we'll light the charcoal."

I left the galley and headed for the bow. Things were sort of quiet, and most of the crew was either in the bunkroom or lounging in the shade. Being I was a surfer dude, I wanted to work on my tan, so I took off my shirt and leaned on the railing. The weather couldn't have been better—mid-eighties and the ocean was so calm it looked like slick grease. The bow cutting through the water sent a mist of salty clean air into my nostrils and stimulated my inner soul. I looked into the deep greenish-blue sea that seemed to have no bottom, and drifted away in thought.

I was paddling out on my board at one of my favorite surfing spots, Lunada Bay. I loved big waves, and when all the other local spots were closed out due to size, the Bay was the place to go. A huge storm out of Alaska had pushed some of the largest recorded waves down the coast of California, and I was determined to ride them.

I was paddling over the shoulder of a big one, when I saw this guy taking off on the next wave. It was huge, maybe twenty feet. He was flying down the face of the wave and made his turn at the bottom. As he reached the top of the crest he started to cut back down this curling monster. The crest of the wave caught up with him, slapped him off his board, and he went tumbling down the face of the wave. It seemed forever before his head popped up in the soup. I realized that I had been holding my breath throughout this wipeout. I thought that maybe I was testing myself to see if I could hold my breath long enough if I wiped out.

I worked my way out to the break and waited for the next set. It wasn't long before I spotted some big swells rolling in. I let the first two waves go by and picked the third. I swung my board around and started to paddle like hell. The first sensation was like going up a fast elevator, then I was on my feet and screaming down the face of the biggest wave I had ever ridden. I made a long sweeping turn at the bottom and positioned myself to stay ahead of the break that was catching up with me, and than I was in the tube. I braced myself for the worst but fortunately the surfing gods were with me. I came shooting out, made a few turns, and pulled out. My heart was pounding so fast I thought I was going to have a stroke.

I rode a couple of smaller waves, and started to paddle out for another big set. The set looked bigger, and that meant it would break farther out. I started paddling as fast as I could, and barely made it over the first one of these waves over twenty-five feet high. I paddled toward the shoulder and made it over. I got through and was totally exhausted. I looked around then realized that I was alone. *Jesus, all those guys must have got caught inside. Man I hope they're OK.*

I had this creepy feeling, then—very alone, distant. I didn't like it, and I couldn't shake it. Another set was rolling in, and I let them go by. Was I scared? Nah, bullshit, not me. Yeah, no shit I was, and I thought maybe it was time to go in. The next swell wasn't too big, so I took it and rode it as far as I could, then paddled to shore.

Wow! I wonder what made me think of that? Maybe I'm a little homesick.

I lit up a cigarette and spotted a school of dolphins. We were headed right through their path. They are such beautiful animals, so sleek and fast, jumping over ten feet in the air. Most people think dolphins perform only in captivity, but in the wild, they were jumping and twisting just for the fun of it. We were now in the middle of the school, and they were playing in front of the bow, shooting one way and another. I watched them until I finished my smoke, then went to the bunkroom.

I spent the next couple of hours reading a Louis L'Amour western. I looked at my watch; it was time to go help John with lunch. When I got to the main deck, I found John loading the barbecue with charcoal.

"Hey, Andy, get the lighter fluid. It's over there."

I grabbed the can and started soaking the charcoal, then I pulled out my Zippo and lit it up. When I was sure the coals were burning good, I headed for the galley to give John a hand.

Everybody loves barbecued chicken, and when we started grilling there was no need to ring the dinner bell, because the enticing aroma drew the whole crew to the table. Even the finicky assholes Ed and Jack, showed up.

I was turning the pieces of chicken when dad came by. "Looks good. Nice of you to give John a hand."

"You know I love to barbecue, and I enjoy helping John. Looks like the crew is in good sprits."

"Well, you know, sitting in Ponce doesn't make them any money."

"I didn't think about that. Need to catch the fish to get

paid. Well. We're off and running, and the weather couldn't be better. Earlier I was on the bow checking out the dolphins, I couldn't believe how calm it was."

"Well enjoy it, because we're in for some nasty weather, starting tonight or early in the morning." The captain smiled at me and walked toward the galley. He turned and said, "Don't burn the chicken. Talk to you later."

I thought John and I prepared way too much food for lunch, but when everybody was finished there wasn't a morsel of food left. Everybody was in a great mood, probably because we had started a new trip and would be fishing soon.

Carlos stood and raised his glass, "Compliments to the cooks." Everyone joined in, then we sat and talked about fishing, told a few jokes, and just had a great time. The captain informed the crew about the expected bad weather. He told Carlos to make sure that everything was secure on deck and to come up to the bridge to go over the watch duty list.

When out to sea, there was always someone standing watch, usually in two-hour intervals on the bridge, twenty-four hours a day. The watch responsibilities consisted of making sure we stayed on course, although most of the time we ran on automatic pilot. Also to be alert to any other boats in the area, any logs or debris floating that could damage the hull if we hit it, and of course, always on the lookout for fish.

By 4:00, we had checked and secured everything on deck, so I decided to go up to the pilothouse and see when my turn at the helm would be. I found the list, and my turn started at 2:00 A.M. Bummer.

I walked over to the captain's quarters and knocked on the door. "Who is it?"

"It's Andy."

Red Sky Morning

"Come on in, son."

Dad was at his desk, doing some paperwork. "How's it going?"

"Well, I needed to wrap up some of the canneries' reports on weights and pricing information, then review all the bills to see how much money we made. Now I'll start concentrating on this trip. I just got the current weather report, and it's gonna blow, starting around six, and last around twenty-four hours."

"That's great; my watch starts at two in the morning."

"Don't worry about it. I'll probably be up and about most of the night. This storm is going to bring a lot of rain, and the wind velocity is expected to be forty plus. You better get some rest while you can, because it will be hard to stay in your bunk later."

I really pigged out at lunch, probably ate a whole chicken, plus a plateful of John's Croatian/Greek salad, half a loaf of fresh baked bread, and a couple of glasses of vino. It was nearing dinnertime, and I was still full from lunch, so I decided to take the captain's advice and get some sleep. I was on deck, walking towards the bunkroom and noticed that the wind was picking up, and the ocean was getting choppy. I jumped into my bunk, and the rocking and rolling put me right to sleep.

I felt someone shacking me, but then I realized it was the *Ace* getting knocked around by a very angry sea. The wind was whistling through everything that wasn't sealed tight. I looked at my watch, it was one fifteen. Forty-five minutes from now I'd be on watch, and I wasn't looking forward to it.

I stayed in my bunk for another fifteen minutes, but I was getting knocked around so much that I decided to get up and get ready for my turn at the helm. I opened the door to get on deck, and the wind and water pushed it shut. I tried again, got on deck and headed for the ladder.

Fortunately, that area of the main deck is partially protected from the sea. Hanging onto the rail, I got to the ladder and climbed up to the bridge as quick as I could. Jesus was on watch, and my dad was right next to him.

"Hey, Dad, what's up?"

"It's really shitty out there. Thought I should stand by."

"Hey, Jesus, I'm early, so I might as well take over."

"Gracias. It's OK, Captain?"

"Sure. Buenas noches, and be careful on deck; you could get washed overboard."

"Si, I be careful. See you *manaña."*

"Jesus is a good man, and so is his brother, Manual. They've have worked for me for over two years."

"Yeah, they're hard workers, and everybody really likes them. Man, it's really rough out there."

Just as I spoke, we hit a huge wave that broke over the bow. The water covered the deck below us.

"I see what you mean about getting washed overboard."

"It can happen even if you're careful. Best thing is to stay inside when the weather's like this."

"How long do you think this storm will last?"

"It should blow through by noon tomorrow, and I think the worst is already over."

"This boat seams to handle the weather pretty good."

"The *Ace* and the *King* are converted seagoing tugs, built by the United States Navy. They were designed to handle bad weather conditions like this."

"When would it be considered too rough?"

"Were riding out a tropical storm, where winds range from forty to sixty miles an hour. Anything above that is considered a hurricane."

"Aren't there different levels of hurricanes?"

"Yeah, they're measured by wind velocity. Category 1

would have sixty to seventy-five miles per hour winds, Category 5 would be 150 plus."

"When would you alter your course to avoid bad weather?"

"Anything worse than this gets critical, and any boat or ship would try to navigate around it or run away from it".

"Have you ever been caught in a hurricane?"

"Yeah, I've been in three or four *Chubascos* in Mexican waters."

"Aren't a chubasco, typhoon and a hurricane the same thing?"

"Yeah, they're all cyclonic type storms."

"How do they start?"

"Well, we're in the Atlantic, let's talk about hurricanes.

Just then, I spotted a giant wave cresting. "Dad!"

Before I could say anything else, he said, "Give me the wheel." All I could see was this black wall with the crest at least level with the bridge coming straight at the bow.

"Hang on."

He slowed the *Ace* as we fell to the bottom of the trough, and then pushed the throttles to full speed when we headed up the face of the wave. The top third of the wave broke over the bow and slammed into the bridge. We got knocked around a little, and the *Ace* shook from the impact, but everything seemed to hold together.

"Jesus Christ! I've seen some rogue waves before, but not this big. That fucking wave was over fifty feet. You better go down and see if everybody's OK. Be careful going down, and don't leave the sheltered part of the deck. There could be another wave like that out there."

"God, I hope not. I'll call you from the galley phone and let you know how everything is."

I went to the bunkroom first. Manuel and Juan had been thrown out of their bunks and were on the deck. They were shook up, but OK.

"What the hell happened?" Manuel asked.

"We got slammed by a rogue wave. It must have been fifty feet high."

Carlos was out of his bunk, already had his pants on, and was pulling up his boots. "I'll go check out the gear. Andy, check out the engine room and the galley."

I climbed down into the engine room and looked around. Everything seemed to be in order, so I headed for the galley. John was already cleaning up, and Carlos walked in from the rear deck. "Everything's OK outside. How about the engine room?"

"I couldn't see anything out of place, and no leaks."

I picked up the phone and rang the bridge. "Hi, son. How's everything?"

"Carlos checked all the gear, and I checked out the engine room, and everything looks OK. Manuel and Juan got thrown out of their bunks, but no one got injured."

"That's good news. Come on back up."

Before I left the galley, I got a couple of cups of coffee and returned to the bridge. "I thought you might like some coffee."

"Thanks, son"

We stood there looking out into the storm as if we were waiting for another rogue wave to appear. Dad pulled out a cigar and bit the tip off. He pulled out his Zippo, and I pulled out a cigarette, then he lit them both up.

"Before that wave hit us, you were going to tell me where a hurricane comes from."

"That's right." He took a pull from his cigar and blew out a plume of smoke. "Well, let's start in the jungles of West Africa, where it's hot and extremely humid. The moisture builds up on the leaves of all the trees that cover the jungle floor. A droplet develops, and when it gets too heavy, the drop falls like rain on the vegetation below. Now, this particular day, the humidity and temperature were much higher than normal. The morning turned into the hottest part of the day and steam began to rise off the jungle's dense vegetation. Under normal conditions, the umbrella type trees would lock up most of the moisture, and the cycle would repeat itself, creating its own microclimate.

"But this particular day, it was extremely hot and humid and the moisture evaporated quickly, and was pulled through the trees towards the glaring sun. Small clouds started to form. As you know, condensation is a common phenomenon, but this day it was happening way too fast. The clouds filled up with moisture so quickly that you could literally see them changing from puffy white to dark and moisture-laden. The rapid formation of these clouds and the constant hot air rising caused this massive formation to move and start to swirl. As it swirled, it started to suck up colder air from the Atlantic, which seem to aggravate the now ugly dark clouds, causing them to spin from the inside out.

"This mass of clouds was rapidly forming into a cyclonic storm, and as it began to spin faster it began to move, feeding on all the moisture it could absorb. It moved toward the coast and became bigger, spinning faster. This tropical depression was rapidly gaining strength. The barometer was dropping around this storm, and it was forming its own identity.

In fact, this is about the time our National Weather Service would give it a name. Let's call this one Andrew, the first hurricane of the season. As Andrew continued to build, it began to cross the Atlantic, heading toward the Caribbean Islands. By this time, Andrew was over four hundred miles wide with a wind velocity of one hundred and twenty miles per hour and growing."

"How big can the waves get in the middle of the Atlantic?"

"A storm this big could create waves fifty to eighty feet high, maybe even bigger."

"What would you do if you got caught in something like that?"

"Pray a lot.

"Many years ago, I got caught in a Chubasco outside of Manzanillo. We were trying to get into port but we were about eighty to ninety miles out when the hurricane hit us. The waves were thirty to forty feet high, and we were in a ninety-foot boat."

"What did you do?"

"Well, the most important thing, is to always make sure you're heading into the swell, and to avoid getting caught broadside. You see, if one of those waves catches you broadside, it could swamp you, and unless you were really lucky you would probably sink. So, you reduce your speed and keep the waves at your bow, and pray you make it."

"Was that the worst storm you were ever in?"

"Out to sea, yes, but about two years later we got an early warning of a huge Chubasco, Category five-type, heading our way. We were fairly close to shore and headed for Xijuatanejo Bay for cover. There was a small fishing village in the bay with little protection for a boat our size. So we anchored right below some cliffs on the east side of the bay. There were four or five other purse seiners anchored in the same area. The hurricane was headed in a westerly direction, and we hoped the cliffs would protect us from the wind."

"It must have been scary just sitting there waiting for the storm to hit."

"Yeah it was. We anchored around nine in the morning, and the weather was great. The crew re-checked all the equipment and rigging, and made sure everything was secure. The lunch bell rang, and we all ate and drank wine, told sea stories, played cribbage and pinochle to pass the time."

I lit up another cigarette and blew out a steady stream of smoke. Dad's Havana burned out while he was talking, so he re-lit it, drew in a couple of puffs, and continued telling the story.

"It was around five or so when the weather started to change. Things got very quiet, and the air became still. It seemed to become more humid. Clouds started to flow over the cliffs, and they appeared to be moving faster than normal. By seven, we had some rainfall, sporadic, and not too heavy. The sun was starting to set on the other side of the bay. At first, it looked like the start of a beautiful sunset. Then the wind started to intensify, and the clouds began to swirl and turn darker. The angry clouds overtook the sun before it set, and the sky became a swirling mass of clouds with colors of a rainbow spinning within them. A rainbow is a beautiful sight, but this angry mass of power spinning above did only one thing. It scared the hell out of us.

"The wind began to pick up; we could hear it whistling through the trees above us. I was relieved that we made the right decision to anchor under the cliffs because they were definitely protecting us from this monster of a storm.

"It was around midnight, and no one on board was sleeping or in their bunk. It started to rain very heavy, and the wind felt like it doubled in force. It was pouring, but none of the rain was actually landing on us.

"The wind was so strong that the rain was going sideways. It was an unbelievable sight. It was like looking at a waterfall if you stood behind it. There wasn't a whistling sound any more, but an ear-blasting roar above. Most of us took shelter in the galley, because a lot of debris was flying around.

Your uncle came running in yelling he just saw a huge tree in one piece — roots and all — fly over the boat. He looked terrified and was mumbling something about the end of the world. All of a sudden, we heard a loud thunk on the deck. Your uncle and I went out to see what happened. To our amazement, there was a full-grown goat lying half-dead on our deck. We put it out of its misery and started to throw it overboard, when the cook yelled, 'let's keep it! If we make it through this, I'll barbecue it and we'll get good and drunk.'

"The cook and two crewmen dressed and cleaned the goat and put it in the refrigerator. When the storm finally passed through, we invited the crews from the other boats that were on anchor and had one hell of a party.

Vince Gillette, captain of one of the boats, yelled, "This goat must have come from heaven, because it's delicious. I want to make a toast. To Andy, for inviting us, and to this goat, and to the cook who prepared it for us."

We all cheered and drank wine, then Vince clicked his glass, with his fork. 'One other thing. I think we should bow our heads and thank God for protecting us, and pray for all those who were hurt or killed because of this devil of a storm.' We sat quietly, then in unison, said, 'Amen.' Then we all commenced to get good and drunk."

"That's quite a story."

"These kinds of experiences make you really respect the sea and the weather. They can be beautiful and provide us with fish, so we can earn money and provide for our families, but if you're not careful, they can also kill you."

"I can't believe it, but my watch is almost over."

"Yeah, and the weather is getting a lot better, so I don't think we'll see another one of those rogue waves. In fact, I think I'll get some shuteye. You've got the helm. Good night, son. It was nice to spend some time together."

"Great story. Good night, Dad."

Chapter 9

We were getting closer to the fishing grounds, and I thought I'd go over the characteristics of the *Western Ace*, its crew, and the method they used to catch fish.

The *Western Ace* was a Navy seagoing tug that was converted to a modern day purse seiner. She was 176 feet long and cruised at 11 to 12 knots. Powered by a large diesel engine, she had a load capacity of 800 tons of fish. The crew consisted of fourteen members, the captain, second mate/navigator, chief engineer, an assistant engineer, chef, and nine deckhands.

A purse seiner of this size used a net 5,000 feet long and 270 feet deep to catch the fish. The top of the net had a nylon rope running through it with corks about a foot in diameter attached about five feet apart. The bottom of the net was attached to a chain with large steel rings. Another cable ran through the rings, which provided the weight to keep the bottom of the net down. One end of the cable was attached to a large winch on deck, the other end hooked onto a winch in the skiff. The 12,000-pound skiff was positioned on the stern, partially on a ramp and on top of the stack of net. The skiff was attached via a cable to a quick-release "pelican hook," mounted on deck.

When looking for schools of fish, it wasn't only the lookout up in the sixty-foot-high crow's nest but the whole crew's responsibility to look for fish. When a school of tuna was spotted, things happened quickly. The captain positioned the boat moving alongside the school. The crew got into position, with one crewman standing ready with a sledgehammer, waiting for the command to hit the pelican hook, which released the cable and the skiff.

That was when it got really exciting. At the precise moment, the captain yelled "Mola Mola" which meant "let it go" in Croatian. The sledgehammer slammed down, and the cable went flying. The skiff launched off the stern, dragging the end of the net with it. It was full speed ahead, and the captain tried to encircle the school of tuna. When the boat was close to completing the circle, the captain steered for the skiff to get the other end of the cable.

When both cables were aboard, the crew got the cable on the winch and began to close up the net into a purse. Until the net is pursed, the fish could swim out the bottom or through the opening. A speedboat and one crewman launched right away. The crewman steered toward the opening of the net, and at full speed zig-zagged in the opening until the gap was closed. Many times he lit and threw seal control bombs into the water to scare the tuna back into the net.

When all the rings were bunched up together and lifted over the rail and secured, the purse was finally closed tight, and the fish had no way to escape. One end of the net was put through the power block (a large hydraulically-powered pulley) then most of the crew positioned themselves on the stern to stack up the mile-long net.

When most of the net was on board, the crew prepared to bunch up the balance, leaving the tuna in it and between the hulls of the boat and the skiff.

Then it was time to load the fish onto the boat and stow them away. To get the fish out of the net the crew used a large scoop net (called a brailer) that held around five tons of fish. The steel hoop is around ten feet in diameter, welded to a twenty-foot-long steel pole. The hoop had two cables attached, one on either side, the other ends attached to a ring. A cable with a hook at the end was lowered and hooked to the ring. The winch man wrapped the cable around the head and controlled lifting and lowering the brailer.

Some of the crew guided the brailer into the opening of the net then pushed the brailer down into the fish and scooped out as much as they could. The brailer was raised over the rail and lowered to the deck. The end of the scoop net had a quick release on it, so when released, the fish poured onto the deck. Half-round chutes were connected and routed to one of twenty wells, and the crew pushed the fish down the chutes to the wells and into a freezing brine.

After all the fish were stowed and the balance of the net stacked, the speedboat was pulled up and secured, and the skiff was pulled up on the stern. That completed a "set," which is really exciting, lots of hard work, and considered one of the most dangerous jobs in any business, plus there was no guarantee that you would catch any fish.

* * *

By the next morning, the storm was gone, and the ocean was calming down. We were in constant communication with the other boats heading for the same area. Roy Katnic, captain of the *Chicken of the Sea,* told my dad that they had already reached the area and made a few sets, one producing seventy-five tons of tuna. That was good news since we were about twelve hours running time from that vessel. Dad decided to head for the fishing area instead of first going to port for additional fuel. We were finally going fishing, and maybe make some money.

We ran all night to reach the fishing area. It was around 6:00 A.M. when we spotted the *Chicken of the Sea,* and our sister-ship, the *Western King.* The *King* was making a set.

"Hopefully, they'll bring in lots of tuna," said my dad.

"Why don't you give them a call?"

"I will, but let's give them a chance to bring in the net, then we'll know how much fish they caught."

They caught forty tons in that set, and that there were good signs of fish in the area.

We immediately went on the prowl, looking for schools of tuna. About an hour went by, and we hadn't spotted a thing. I was on the bridge looking through a pair of binoculars when I thought I spotted something on the horizon. I focused the binoculars, and then I was certain that there was a bunch of birds circling an area.

"There's a bunch of birds circling over there," I yelled to my Dad.

He grabbed his binoculars and looked where I was pointing, then turned the boat in that direction and kicked it ahead to full speed. I knew that birds circling or a school of porpoise jumping could mean a school of tuna underneath them. The crewman in the crow's nest confirmed my sighting and added that there was tuna below them. I was really proud of myself, and it made me feel like part of the crew. Carlos told everyone to get into position.

"Mola Mola!" yelled the man from the crow's nest. The sledgehammer came down on the pelican hook, and we were in the middle of making our first set of the trip. My assignment was manning the speedboat. I had practiced while we were in Puerto Rico, but this was the real thing, and suddenly I felt alone. I lowered the boat into the water, jumped on, started the engine, and took off at full speed. I was so excited that I lost my bearings. I looked back at the *Western Ace,* and I could see my father waving at me and pointing toward the opening in the net; I was way off course. Man, was I embarrassed. I spun the boat around and headed for the opening. When I got there (seemed like it took forever), I started to run back and forth between ends of the open net. I could see tuna jumping inside the net, and it looked like they were headed my way. *Oh shit, they're going to swim right through the opening.* I pushed the throttle to full speed (about thirty knots) and started zigzagging and spinning the boat back and forth. The tuna stopped jumping and there were no signs of fish on the surface. *God, I hope the tuna didn't swim out.*

The opening in the net was closing rapidly, and my father waved and motioned that I should come in. I pulled the boat under the davits, hooked up the lines, and climbed out. I prayed that I'd done my job right.

It was time to start bringing in the net. We all took positions on the stern, got a hold on the net, and got ready to restack it. The power block turned and pulled the net up out of the water and down to us. It took about twenty-five minutes to stack the net.

One of the crew yelled, "We got fish!"

We carefully bunched up the net, with one side attached to the skiff and the other to the *Ace.* This way the net would stay open at the top, and we could start brailing the fish and dumping them into the wells.

Carlos slapped me on the shoulder and said, "You did real good out there."

He had no idea how relieved I felt.

I couldn't believe it. We'd only been in the fishing area for about six hours, and we had over fifty tons of tuna on board. Hell, at this rate I might get a little surfing in before school started.

We cleaned up, got the gear ready for the next set, and went looking for more fish. A couple of hours went by when a school of porpoise were spotted. " Mola mola!" and we were off and running. After most of the net was in, I realized it was empty. I started to understand why it took thirty or forty days to load up

Chapter 10

We continued looking for tuna off the coast of West Virginia and Maryland and headed west. It was getting late in the day, and my dad decided to head for Delaware's port to take on fuel and provisions.

We entered the port and dropped anchor around six. A few minutes later, the cook rang the bell; it was time for dinner, and I was starving. Everyone was taking their seats when Ed, the new engineer, blurted out, "So what kind of shit are you serving us tonight?"

We could tell he'd had been drinking and was totally out of line. This wasn't the first time he had shown up drunk. In fact, my father had previously warned him and his assistant about drinking during the day and causing problems with the rest of the crew.

Alberto jumped up and started moving toward the engineer. He was pissed and started cursing in Spanish. The rest of the crew stood up in support of the cook. They started yelling for the engineer and his assistant to get out of the galley. Just when I thought the fists would start flying, my father walked in. He realized what was going on and yelled at them to stop.

He glared at the engineer, and said, "Get your ass over here." They went out on deck, and the captain chewed his ass out, giving him a final warning. If he didn't straighten out he would be finished on this boat. Ed wandered off with Jack, the assistant.

The rest of us sat down for dinner. What a spread. For appetizers, we had pickled tongue, shrimp, cheese, cold cuts, and fresh baked bread. Dinner consisted of a roast pork loin, a spicy chicken stew, Portuguese-style, grilled vegetables, broiled potatoes with garlic, and a mixed salad. My dad, the second mate, Frank Kastransich, and I are Croatian. Other than the two drunks, we and the rest of the crew loved John's European and spicy style of cooking.

There was plenty of food and wine on the table, and we were all in good sprits. We finished dinner and helped John clear and wash the dishes. We decided to play gin rummy, so we broke up into teams, set the amount at twenty-five cents a point, and played till past midnight.

The next morning everybody slept in a little longer than normal, because the captain gave us the morning off. I loved to sportfish, and brought out the rod and reel I used when we were in Puerto Rico.

I went down to the galley and got some frozen squid from John to use for bait. I went up on deck, tied on a hook and sinker, put on a piece of squid and cast out about thirty feet. It didn't take long before I felt a bite. I set the hook, and the fish put up a good fight. It turned out to be a striped bass, weighing around fifteen pounds. I was ecstatic because striped bass was considered a delicacy, and if I could catch three or four, we would have fresh fish for dinner.

My dad walked up to see how I was doing. He was surprised to see a striped bass in the bucket next to me, and said, "Catch a couple more, and we'll have them for dinner."

I said, "I already told the cook. I hope that doesn't give

me any bad luck." He laughed and told me he was going to a meeting, and would be back in two or three hours.

About ten minutes later, I got a strike and tried to set the hook, but I missed him. "Shit." I reeled in the line, put a fresh piece of bait on and cast it in the same area. Just as the bait hit the water, a fish boiled on it. I let him take some line, counted to three, and set the hook. I was sure this one was bigger than the first fish because it was pulling out line with the same drag setting as the first fish I caught. It took about ten minutes to bring it to the side of the boat.

It was definitely a bigger striper, and I knew I couldn't bounce him onto the deck. I yelled to John, who I knew was in the galley. He came out running.

"What you catch?"

"Another striper. Could you get the gaff and bring it in?"

"Sure." John grabbed the gaff and got close to the fish. He took a swipe at it and missed. The fish spooked and sounded, peeling line off the reel. John cussed in Croatian, and looked at me. "Sorry, bring him up, I try again."

I got him back to the side of the boat, and this time John didn't miss. He looked at me with a big grin, and said, "Looks like we got enough for dinner. I go clean both of them." The second striper weighed over twenty five pounds. I couldn't believe it.

John went back to the galley, which was a level below the main deck. I put on more bait and continued to fish. I heard a splash below me and saw a large white package floating in the water. A second later, I could hear John screaming, "What the hell you think you're doing?"

"Ah, shut up, you fucking foreigner. I'm sick and tired of the food around here."

It was Ed, and you could tell he was drunk and had totally lost it. More packages were going overboard; I couldn't believe what I was seeing. John and Ed were screaming at each other.

"You son of a bitch, I'm gonna kill you," John yelled.

I could hear things crashing on the deck below me, and then I heard someone running up the stairs. It was Ed, and he had a terrified look on his face. I could understand why, because right behind him, crazy mad, was John, swinging a meat clever and yelling, "You bastard, I'm gonna cut your balls off."

They were running around the deck cussing at each other. It was almost comical looking, but I was sure that if the cook caught the drunk, he might carry out his threat.

By now, the rest of the crew was on deck watching and laughing at the two. Suddenly, John had the engineer cornered on the bow, and it stopped being funny. The cook swung. The drunk ducked, and the cleaver missed Ed's head by an inch, slamming into the railing. Ed's eyes were wide with fear, and John was screaming and raising the meat clever over his head. The engineer took one look at that blade, turned, and leaped over the side. Everybody started laughing and watched the drunk swim to shore. He never set foot on our deck again.

I didn't know what business my father went to shore for, but later I found out that he had hired a new engineer and an assistant. We were in the galley when he got back and made the announcement.

"By the way, have any of you seen Ed?" We all started laughing and told him about the earlier incident.

"Too bad you didn't catch him, John. All that food he threw overboard cost a lot of money. What an asshole," Dad said.

The new engineer and his assistant were flying out from the West Coast the following day, and we planned to leave as soon as they arrived. Kenny, the new engineer, and Jack, his assistant were on the boat by 11:00 A.M. We pulled up the anchor and headed for the open sea. We had lunch, where my dad introduced the two engineers to the rest of the crew.

Chapter 11

During the time we were in port, the fleet moved farther north, so we headed in that direction, expecting to catch up within twenty-four hours. Around six, my dad radioed the *Western King*. The skipper told him they had just spotted some tuna fifteen minutes earlier and hoped to make a set soon. This was good news, because the whole fleet had not made a set since we went into port.

At 9:00 P.M. we received a message for Juan and Raul that their father was close to death and had requested that they be at his side. They asked permission to leave the *Ace* and go home. Of course, my dad said OK. Juan and Raul were both good workers and would be missed.

When the fleet decided to fish the East Coast, the owners put a list together of contacts on the Eastern seaboard that could assist them in providing goods and services required while fishing in that area. Now that we had lost two crew members, we needed to find replacements. We were in luck. The owner of a large fish brokerage house in Rhode Island knew of three college students looking for summer jobs, which would work perfectly. We could head back to port, drop off Juan and Raul, and pick up the new guys. At the end of summer, the three students would leave, and the *Ace* would head back to the Pacific so Juan and Raul could meet the boat in Panama.

Although the crew was great and we had fun, most of them spoke little English and they were all older. I thought it would be great to have some guys on the boat that I could relate to.

We went into port to pick them up, and they were waiting on the dock. We really didn't need anything because we had loaded up on fuel, water, and provisions two days ago. After the guys got aboard, we headed out to sea.

The new guys were great, and we hit it off immediately. It was my turn to introduce them to the crew, and it seemed that there was an immediate acceptance. The captain asked me to show them around, explain how we caught fish, and what their duties would be. This was a real challenge, because little did they know that I was just a rookie. Their names were Casey, John, and Doug. They had just started college at Rhode Island State and were planning to play football that season. I couldn't believe it. I also played, and my team was all-city champs. Our quarterback was named All-American, and was on the cover of Sports Illustrated. From that point on we were buddies.

They were very attentive as I explained their duties to them. I stressed how dangerous it was while we were making a set, and that they had to keep alert at all times. They had a million questions; I think I answered them adequately. We would find out soon enough, because we were only three hours away from the fleet. My dad just finished talking to the skipper on the *Chicken of the Sea,* who informed him that there was a good sign of tuna in the area and that most of the fleet had made a set or two and had fish on board.

Red Sky Morning

We were getting close to the fleet, and the guys asked me to go over their jobs with them again. I asked Carlos to join in on the conversation. We went step-by-step, going into detail when necessary.

"Well, you think you're ready"?

Casey looked at John and Doug, and they all nodded yes. I felt the boat surge forward and knew we'd gone from cruising to full speed ahead. I looked at the guys and said, "Well, it looks like you'll find out in a few minutes."

Carlos jumped up, ran to the rail, and pointed toward the bow.

"Porpoise."

The captain turned hard right, and we could all see a huge school of porpoise jumping and running in the same direction we were. "You better get ready," Carlos said.

Casey's job was working in the skiff, while John and Doug were to help with the rigging and stack the net. We all moved to our positions and waited. The boat made a turn to the left. "Mola mola!"

We were off and running. I watched the skiff slide off the stern rail and slam into the water, and I could see the whites of Casey's eyes. I'm sure he didn't expect everything to move so quickly.

The captain completed the circle, and I was getting ready to launch the speedboat. It was time, so I lowered the boat into the water, released the ropes, and fired up the engine. I headed for the opening at 30 knots, and started to run back and forth. I had a bunch of seal control bombs with me, a lit cigar between my lips, and one hand on the wheel. With the other hand I grabbed a seal control, which was as strong as a quarter stick of dynamite, lit the fuse, and threw it overboard.

I continued tossing the bombs as fast as I could. It was like dropping mini depth charges, except they were not designed to damage the seals or fish, but to scare the fish, hopefully, back into the net.

Everything went like clockwork, and we were almost finished stacking the net, when I heard my dad say, "Looks like we got some fish." He seemed pretty excited and ordered the crew to get ready to brail the fish out. The net was pursed up tight, and it was loaded with tuna, so we got back to work.

Doug looked over at me and said, "This is hard work, but man it's sure exciting. I can't believe there's so much fish in the net." He was right. In that set, we caught over eighty tons of tuna.

We had over 130 tons on board and needed about 600 tons to load up. At the rate we were going, I thought it shouldn't take too long. There was still some daylight and we were on the move, looking for more fish. It didn't take long before we spotted more porpoise and shortly after, the spotter in the crows nest was yelling "Mola!" I started to realize just how hard this job can be. We had just broken our buts, bringing in eighty tons of tuna and had little rest before we were at it again. I also found how disappointing fishing can be, because when we finished this set there weren't any fish in the net. It was even more disappointing when Carlos said, "You know, sometime we make four or five sets in one day and don't catch any fish."

The dinner bell was ringing, so we all cleaned up and went to the galley. As usual, John put out a huge spread. "Man, this food is fabulous," said Casey, and everyone agreed. We ate and drank and talked about the day. The guys were all pumped up about their new jobs and were looking forward to the next day. We sat around the table for an hour or so, but most everyone was tired so we all turned in to our bunks.

Someone is on watch twenty-four hours a day. Of

course, during the day the captain or second mate were at the helm, constantly looking out for other boats or ships in our path. At night, crew members took a two-hour shift either at the helm or when the boat was adrift. My shift started at 4:00 A.M., which meant I would go straight to work the next morning. The crew let the new guys off for that night, but their turns would come up.

After three days out to sea, we had made nine more sets, but only three were productive. We added about sixty more tons to our catch. The following day was my seventeenth birthday. My shift started at 6:00 A.M., and when I walked onto the bridge my dad who was listening to the weather report turned, "Hey son, happy birthday. How does it feel to be a year older?"

"Good . . . Hey dad, I told the guys I was turning eighteen. They're starting college and I—you know . . ."

"I understand. My lips are sealed."

There was a hurricane building up off of Florida, and it looked as if it might head further north.

Fishing wasn't that good, and we were a little low on fuel, so my dad decided to head for port in Providence Rhode Island.

The engineer needed some parts for the refrigeration system and radioed ahead to place the order. The parts had to be shipped from California and would take three days to get here. This meant we would be in port for at least four days.

We celebrated my seventeenth birthday at dinner, and John baked a cake for desert. We drank more wine than we should have, and played cards till midnight. The next day we would be in port where the drinking age was eighteen. I looked as old as the other guys, *God I hope I don't get caught. How embarrassing would that be?*

Chapter 12

The college guys were all excited because they went to school there and were ready to party, and of course, so was I. Doug had left his car at their fraternity house, so we planned to pick up the car and see what was going on around campus. Since it was summer, there wasn't much happening, but we ran into one of their fraternity brothers, who told us about a new club called RJ's that had just opened and was packed every night. This was good news, so we screwed around at the fraternity house until it was time to go party.

We got to RJ's a little early, went to the bar, and got some beers. We were all eighteen. At least that's what everyone thought, so buying liquor wasn't a problem. Casey spotted one of his friends and called him over. Casey introduced me to Ronnie, who asked, "So you work on this boat?"

"Yeah, just for summer break, then back to L.A." We talked about California, Hollywood, and surfing.

"You look like a surfer."

I was six-three and weighed 240. I thought I looked

more like a football player than a surfer. In actuality, I was both; I guess it was my long blondish hair and dark tan.

Ronnie said, "You should do well with the women around here, because they're crazy about California surfer guys. It might be slow tonight because there's a big beach party going on."

Let's go there," said Casey. Ronnie asked Casey to drive with him, and John and I went with Doug.

We stopped at a liquor store and picked up a case of beer. It took twenty minutes to get to the beach, and there were over a hundred people there. A band was playing, "Let's Go Surfing" by the Beach Boys. *This is right up my alley.* We started to mingle, Casey asked this fox to dance, and Doug introduced me to a few of their friends. They were all interested in California, surfer girls, movie stars, etc. When I told them my friends and I hung out and surfed with the Beach Boys in Redondo Beach, I thought they were going to ask for my autograph. I realized what a craze California and surfing was on the East Coast, and knew I could take advantage of it.

It was time to check out the action, so I started to walk around and see what was happening. I spotted three lookers standing by one of the fires. One of them was really bitchin, and I hoped she liked to dance. When I walked up to her and asked, she smiled and nodded. The band started playing one of my favorites, "Wipe Out" by the Surfaris. We were dancing away, and she yelled at me, "You're not from here are you?"

My chance, "No, I'm from California"

"Oh really, what area?"

"The beach, near Los Angeles."

"I knew it. You dance differently, I mean not bad, but really good"

"I'll bet you're a surfer."

Red Sky Morning

    I nodded, she smiled. She had beautiful eyes, long blonde hair, and a great body to go with it. She reminded me of the girls back home except lacking a good tan.
    The band stopped playing and announced that they were taking a break. Perfect timing. She smiled and asked, "What's your name?"
    "Andy"
    "Hi, my name is Lauren. Come on, I want you to meet my girlfriends."
    They were all good-looking, and thrilled to meet a California surfer guy. Casey and Ronnie walked up, and I introduced them. Ronnie passed out some beers, and we were all having a great time. The band started up again, and we all danced.
    The third song was a slow one. I was looking forward to this. I put my arm around Lauren's waist, and she put both of hers around my neck and pulled me close to her. *God, it's been a long time.* I could feel her boobs rubbing against my chest, and it felt so good. Uh-oh, I was getting a hard-on, how embarrassing. The more I wanted it to go away, the harder it got. I think she felt it, because she moved back a little. Now we were looking at each other. I could feel my face getting hot, and I'm sure a little red. She had beautiful green eyes, and they were focused on mine. It was as if she were analyzing me, which made me feel uncomfortable. I thought I should say something, but just as I began to speak she smiled and drew me close, very close, to her.
    It felt so good, and I wished the band would keep playing, but they finally finished. Lauren didn't let go. The band started playing a fast song, but we were still dancing cheek to cheek. I moved back a little, gazed into her eyes and had a sudden urge to kiss her, so I did. She responded positively and time stood still, while a hundred other people

around us were a-rockin' and a- rollin.'

I don't know how long we kissed, but it seemed like a long time. Lauren whispered into my ear, "You want to take a walk on the beach?" Of course, my answer was yes.

We took our shoes off and walked into the darkness. The sand felt good on my feet. I began to think about surfing back home, and how much I missed it. Lauren asked, "What are you thinking about"? I told her, and she asked, "Is there a girlfriend that goes with those thoughts?"

"Yeah, there is."

"Do you miss her?"

"I think so, but not as much as I thought I would. I called her about a week ago, and she seemed to be having a great summer without me. She talked about the great parties she and her girlfriends were going to, and that they were at the beach almost every day. She asked me if I had met any other women this summer. I told her I hadn't and that most of the time we were at sea fishing. Then I asked if she had met any guys. She said; of course not; just going out with the girls. I'm not convinced, because I know her girlfriends, and I'm sure she's seeing other guys."

"Does that bother you?"

"A little, but right now all I can think of is you."

I wrapped my arms around her and kissed her as passionately as I could. We slowly dropped to the sand, holding that kiss. Before I knew it, we had half our clothes off. It was getting very heavy when Lauren sighed, "I think we better slow down." God, I wanted to continue, but I wasn't going to force myself on her. Hell, I was going to be in port for three more days, so maybe I would get lucky.

We lay there looking at the moon and saying very little. I could feel a bad case of blue balls coming on, and I wasn't looking forward to walking back. Lauren sat up, leaned over, and kissed me.

Red Sky Morning

"Maybe we should get back to the party."

I looked into her green eyes and said, "Will I see you again?"

"You have three more days here, don't you?"

I was going to say yes, but she interrupted me, "I'm busy tomorrow, but how about Saturday?"

I felt like I'd won the lottery. "It's a date. You pick a place to go to dinner and—"

She held up her hand. "My roommate will be gone all weekend, so let's have dinner in." *Well it looks like I'm going to get lucky after all.*

When Lauren and I got back to the party there were only a few people milling around. Lauren spotted her girlfriends, who were still with Casey and Ronnie. They were waiting for us, so we all said our good-byes and left in separate cars.

The next day was business as usual, except I now had a date for tomorrow night. We planned to go to RJ's tonight and party down. We arrived around eight, and the place was jumping. Casey was considered the big butt-man around campus. He spotted a girl he knew and asked her to dance. Doug, John, and I walked over to the bar and got a drink. Doug said, "Andy, look at those girls sitting at the table"

"They look pretty good to me. Let's go."

We grabbed John, walked up to their table and asked if we could join them. They said OK, so we sat down and ordered more drinks. The California surfer thing worked again, and I was a big hit. The girls couldn't stop talking about California, Hollywood, and movie stars. I was loving it! We all talked for a while, and I felt that one of the girls named Judy was coming on to me, so I asked her to dance. John and Doug asked the other two ladies, and they joined in.

Judy was a great dancer, and I was having a ball. I spotted Casey dancing with a different girl than he'd started with, and she was really put together. She had long blonde hair and a body that belonged in a *Playboy* centerfold. Judy poked me and said, "Who are you looking at?"

"Oh, I just spotted my other friend dancing over there"

"Yeah, with that beautiful blonde? You sure you're not just checking her out?"

I didn't know how to respond. *Come on Andy think and be straightforward.* I looked into her eyes and said, "She is good looking, isn't she?" That caught her off guard. I just acted as if it wasn't important and hoped I didn't offend her. I guess I didn't, because the band started playing a slow song, and she asked me to dance.

It looked like all three couples hit it off, and we were having a great time. The girls excused themselves to go to the ladies' room.

"Did you get a look at that girl Casey's with?" John asked.

"Yeah, she's a real fox, isn't she?"

We all agreed that she was the best-looking girl we'd seen in a long time, and what a body. Doug said, "Here come the girls." We all knew where our attention should be focused.

The girls lived together and went to the same school as John and Doug. We were having a great time when Casey came over to the table. "I'm leaving with my new girlfriend, so I'll see you guys in the morning." He had a shitass grin on his face, and he was loving every minute of it, that lucky shit.

About an hour later, we were about ready to leave and go to a coffee shop, when out of nowhere, Casey was standing at our table. He looked terrible, his clothes all disheveled, his perfectly combed hair was a mess, and was white as a ghost. He grabbed the drink out of my hand and

Red Sky Morning

gulped it down.

"God, what happened to you"? asked John.

Casey was truly shaken and was having a hard time speaking. "You won't believe this. After I left your table, we went out to her car. Instead of leaving right away, we started making out. It started to get pretty heavy; I mean she had my pants down to my knees and was giving me a blowjob. I slid my hand into her panties, and when I went for it I found a hard dick. She was a he!"

Casey never got over it. He was still shook up about the incident when I left to go home at the end of August.

Casey wanted to go back to the boat, and we wanted to go with the girls. John's date, Kathy, volunteered to drive us back later, so everything worked out, except Casey's ego. The rest of the evening went better than expected. We ended up going to the girls' house, where we continued to party, ending up in their bedrooms.

On Saturday morning all I could think about was seeing Lauren that evening. I realized that we didn't discuss what time, or how I was going to get to her house. I thought I'd better give her a call. There was a pay phone on the dock, so I went to my bunk, got some change, and made the call.

"Hello, is Lauren there?"

"Sorry, you must have the wrong number. There's no Lauren here." I felt a big knot in my stomach and hung up the phone. *Try again, you dummy. Maybe you really dialed the wrong number.* I put in another dime and dialed again.

"Hello." It was Lauren's voice. The knot in my stomach was quickly replaced by a pounding heart.

"Hello, anybody there?"

"Yeah, hi, it's Andy."

"God, I'm glad you called."

Here it comes, I'm sorry but I can't make it tonight, or

something like that.

"I realized that I didn't give you my address, and that you don't have any wheels. You are planning to come, aren't you?"

"Of course, I'm looking forward to it. As far as the wheels go, I'll take a taxi."

"I'd pick you up, but I have to go shopping for dinner and run some errands. Is five o'clock all right?"

"Perfect, I'll see you then. By the way, I love to cook, and I'll bring the wine."

She sighed. "Sounds like we should have a good time. See you then."

"Great, see ya." I hung up the phone and did a little dance.

I gave the cabbie the address and asked if he would stop at a liquor store and a flower shop before we got there. The stores were about a block apart. I bought some Champagne, a couple of bottles of Cabernet, and I picked up some fresh flowers.

The driver pulled to the curb, and Lauren greeted me at the porch. She looked beautiful, and I told her so. She blushed and kissed me.

Lauren thanked me for the flowers, and I opened the champagne. We had a great time cooking dinner together, and the end result was a sumptuous meal. After dessert, she asked, "Would like an after-dinner drink?"

"Sounds great! What did you have in mind?"

"How about, a Coffee Beautiful?"

"Let's go in the kitchen, and I'll help you make them."

Lauren smiled. "Thanks, but Ill take care of it. Why don't you go into the living room and relax."

Lauren came back with our drinks. "Its delicious," I said. She was standing there, smiling, and she had a little whipped cream on her lips. All I could think of was to lick it off. So I did just that. I set my drink down, put my arms around her, and kissed her, then I licked the whipped cream off her upper lip.

"It's my turn," she said. She got some cream out of her cup and smeared it all over my face, then she slowly started to lick it off. I couldn't take it; I grabbed her and smeared the cream between our lips.

We were on the couch half-undressed, our hands feeling each other's body. She stopped and looked at me. "It just occurred to me that I'll probably never see you again."

Here we go again, another case of blue balls. Shit, I don't know if I can handle it. "I hate to say it, but you're probably right."

She kissed and hugged me passionately, then whispered in my ear, "Is it OK if I take you back to your boat tomorrow morning?"

I'll never forget that moment or the time I spent with Lauren.

Chapter 13

Monday morning we left Rhode Island, and it was hard to get in the fishing mood. As we cruised out to sea, the swells were getting huge. I went up to the bridge to talk to the captain. My father was looking at some navigational charts and looked up. "Hi, son, I heard you had a pretty good time back there."

"It was great."

"Is it true that Casey ended up with a transvestite one night?"

I started laughing. "I couldn't believe it. I don't think he'll ever be the same."

"I'm glad it wasn't you."

"Me too. So, what's with these big swells?"

"Remember that hurricane down south? Well, it's not headed this way, but it's a big storm and even though it's hundreds of miles away, it's creating these swells. They'll get bigger as we get out farther."

Three or four hours went by before we spotted some of the fleet. The swells were gigantic, maybe thirty-five to fifty feet high. They were huge ground swells, and the distance from one peak of one swell to the next was over a half-mile. There wasn't a breath of wind, and it almost felt as if the sea was flat and calm. Of course, if the wind came up with any force, it could get real ugly, even dangerous.

The hurricane not only pushed up the swells but caused the temperature and humidity to go up as well. Most of the crew wore only shorts and tennis shoes. It was a good time to work on a tan, and Casey and the guys were taking advantage of it. We all wore swim trunks and spread tanning lotion all over ourselves. The rest of the crew started making fun of us, holding their noses and saying we smelled like coconuts.

John stepped out of the galley and rang the dinner bell. I was starving, and I guess everyone else was too, because we all got to the galley door at the same time. Everyone was at the table except the skipper and Juan, who was up in the crow's nest, hopefully spotting a school of fish.

Lunch was roasted chicken and risotto, and it smelled great. I was on my second bite of chicken when my dad's voice came on the intercom, "Tuna Tuna! Get to your stations." We all jumped up, and John was mumbling in Croatian, probably upset that lunch was ruined.

You could feel the boat surge forward as the skipper put the pedal to the metal. There was electricity in the air as everyone waited for the word to let it go. The *Ace* made a quick right turn and than came about to the port.

"MOLA MOLA!"

Carlos was all excited, pointing to the portside, *"Mas grande pescado!"* I took that as a big school of tuna. I left my position by the speedboat and ran over to the portside. There were fish jumping and boiling as far as I could see. Carlos looked at me and grinned, his gold tooth glistening in the sunlight. He motioned for me to get back to my spot, which I did immediately.

Red Sky Morning

It was speedboat time, so I lowered my craft into the ocean, jumped on, and fired up the engine. I pushed the throttle to full and headed for my area. All of a sudden, I couldn't see anything but water and sky. Where was the *Ace*? I started to panic, then as fast as the *Ace* disappeared, it was on my port side. I became a little disoriented and was way off of my position. I then realized just how big the swells really were, because as one swell passed under my boat and I was in the trough I couldn't see the *Ace,* its mast, or even the crow's nest. Right at that point, I felt very alone and uneasy. That wasn't like me. Hell, I've been out surfing in twenty-foot waves before, and I admit, it was a little scary, but I loved every minute of it.

The uneasy feeling started to diminish, and I noticed that I was way off course. I spun my boat around and headed for the opening in the net, hoping that I didn't screw anything up. The guys on deck secured the other side of the net, and my job was over so I headed back to the *Ace*. When I got back on deck we were ready to start stacking the net, so I got to my position on the stern. As the net passed through the power block a bunch of scallops fell to the deck.

"I guess the net must have dragged on the bottom," Carlos said.

The cook saw the fresh scallops dropping and yelled, "Throw them to me; I'll cook them for dinner."

Carlos responded, "Cook them? Hell, lets eat them raw or make some ceviche. They gonna taste like candy." John agreed and piled them up in a bucket.

A few minutes later some gooey stuff landed on my shoulder, which immediately started to sting. All at once, the gooey stuff was falling all over everybody, and in a couple of seconds we were all covered with it.

"Jelly fish!" yelled Juan.

"Worse, they're man-of-war jelly fish," said Carlos. I felt like I was on fire. Carlos yelled, "John, get the hose and wash us off. Keep stacking, but don't look up. One at a time, go rinse off and put on some rain gear. And hurry up. We can't stop; we got lots of fish."

Doug yelled, "My eyes, my eyes! God damn, it hurts!"

I saw the first man running back with his rain gear almost on, so I yelled at Doug to go next and wash his eyes out. It was a nightmare happening right before my eyes. We couldn't stop stacking the net, and I could see the welts rising on the backs and faces of the crew. It was my turn to wash off. As hard as John could spray me, I could still feel the venom at work. I got my gear on and pulled the hood over my head, then went back to work. The rain gear protected us from the onslaught of jellyfish, or should I say the Portuguese Man-of-Wars, which are poisonous. Its sting isn't deadly to humans, but its venom can easily kill a small fish.

It was ninety degrees outside, and the relative humidity was over ninety-eight. You can't imagine what it felt like working in that heat with heavy rain gear on. Bad enough, just with the gear, but our skin was on fire, and we could barely stand it. For a moment, I felt that I might pass out. One of the crew fell to his knees and then to his side. My dad ran over, picked him up, and carried him to where John had the hose and started to rip off the rain gear. He soaked him with fresh water, and he came to. We finished stacking the net; as far as we could see the balance was full of tuna. I couldn't believe how much fish we had in the net; it was well over a hundred tons. The rain gear came off, and we got down to business loading the fish. Everybody looked terrible, with big red welts all over their bodies, but the excitement of catching so much fish somehow camouflaged the excruciating pain we all felt.

In that one set we caught over 180 tons of tuna, which

took most of the day to load into the fish wells. We were all exhausted, not only from the work, but from of the jellyfish. We spread on calamine lotion, sprayed on Bactine, and anything else that was soothing, olive oil from the kitchen, and even suntan lotion that smelled like coconuts. We looked funny as hell sitting at the dinner table with all this stuff on our faces, but all the shit we smeared on us relieved a lot of the pain, and most of us started to regain our appetites.

"I think we've had enough today, let's get some rest," Dad said. I could see that everybody was relieved that we wouldn't be making another set or two that afternoon.

Now that we were out to sea we all took shifts standing watch. My shift started at midnight, so I went straight to my bunk to get some sleep. I was exhausted from the day, and the stings were starting to itch, making it hard to fall asleep. I lay there thinking of what I'd experienced in the last two months, definitely a real adventure so far. I thought I would never reach Puerto Rico and would die in a plane crash. I had a great time there, drinking lots of rum and Coke and partying with the crew and the local woman. John, damn near killing the engineer. Partying with Casey and friends, and then there was Lauren. *Man I sure wish I could see her again.*

I felt someone shaking me and whispering, "Andy, wake up, it's time for your watch." I never over-sleep. It's like I have an alarm clock built into my system, but I obviously over-slept that night. I jumped out of my bunk and threw on my clothes, went straight to the galley to get a cup of coffee, then ran up to the bridge to take my shift. Doug, who woke me up, was waiting for me to relieve him. He said, "I haven't seen anything for three hours. It's really pitch-black out there, and these swells look like mountains coming at us."

Doug left, and I was still drowsy, so I stayed outside and walked around so I wouldn't doze off. I heard someone talking, and I realized it was coming from the radio: "*Western King,* calling the *Western Ace.* Andy, you there?" I knew they were calling for my dad, so I went to the captain's quarters to wake him up. My dad's room was next to the radio room, and when I reached for his door knob the door opened up and dad was already on his way to answer the call.

It was the skipper of the *Western King.* He was informing my dad that they were going to move farther north because one of the other boats had spotted a lot of fish just before dark. It was about a four-hour run to where Roy Katnic, captain of the *Chicken of the Sea* spotted the fish, so the two skippers agreed to make the move. Dad came outside and told me that we were making a move. I had to wake up the engineer and tell him to start the engines. When I got back to the bridge, my dad was standing over the chart table. He was plotting our position via the Loran signals, and then he would set the course for our new destination. It took him a few minutes to get ready, then he got on the intercom and told the engineer that he was ready to get underway. He grabbed the wheel and pushed the throttle forward. With the boat on course, He put on the autopilot. "Keep a sharp lookout, because we'll be going through the shipping lanes that run to New York, and there's always some traffic. I still don't trust this new autopilot, check the compass to make sure we stay on course. If you run into any problems take her out of auto and wake me up. Good night."

I had almost two hours left on my shift, and I could hardly keep my eyes open. I scanned the horizon then ran down to the galley for more coffee. There were a couple of stale donuts there, so I took them with me. I ran back up to the bridge and rescanned the area. I couldn't see anything, so I concentrated on the donuts and coffee.

After that little run to the galley, eating two donuts, and drinking a mug of coffee, I felt pretty alert, so I pulled up a stool and sat in front of the steering wheel. The sugar and caffeine started to wear off, and I could feel myself running out of gas. I had about a half-hour to go, so I got up and started to walk around. I spotted some lights a long way in the distance, and they looked like they were headed toward us. They were a long way out, and I didn't pay to much attention to them. Suddenly the lights from the boat were getting bigger and seemed to be coming at us faster.

I realized that it wasn't a boat, but a very large ship coming at us faster than I could imagine. I didn't know if we were on a collision course, and I grabbed the binoculars to see its bow and mast lights. The bow light is lower than the mast light, because if they're lined up on top of each other, you're on a collision course. If this situation occurs at sea, the rules of navigation dictate that both vessels are to bear to starboard. All vessels have running lights, which are mounted on the sides of a boat, with a red light on the portside, and a green light on the starboard. When bearing to starboard, the red light should be visible on the other vessel, because if it's not everyone's in deep shit.

The ship was bearing down on us, and its bow and mast lights were right on top of each other. We were on a collision course, so I turned off the automatic pilot, started blowing the horn, and turned hard to starboard. It seemed like everything went into slow motion, and the ship looked like a mountain coming at me.

"Shit, were going too slow," I yelled and pushed the throttle to full, staring at the oncoming ship.

My father came running out of his room, looked out the window and yelled, "Jesus Christ! Are we going to make it?"

"I don't know. There's nothing more I can do, and it doesn't look like they're turning." *God, why me? Why did I have to be on watch?*

The ship was about a hundred yards from us, moving at twenty knots plus. We were running at twelve, which meant that in just a few seconds, the ship would crash into us.

It might have felt like slow motion before, but not now. All I could see was the bow of that ship towering over us. I looked at my father, who was bracing him self against the wall.

"God, I'm sorry Dad."

"It's not your fault. Hang on!"

I was hanging onto the wheel, and we were turning, but it was too late. It looked like the bow was moving away from us.

My dad yelled, "It's gonna be close!" The bow wave hit us broadside, but fortunately we were turning right, so the wave just knocked us into a sharper turn. I turned the wheel to straighten us out, and looked at my dad, who was smiling. "God damn, that was close. Excuse me while I go change my underwear."

I was laughing and crying at the same time. I knew death had stared right at us, but it just wasn't our time to go.

Within seconds, most of the crew was in the pilothouse wondering what had happened. Doug said, "God, I thought it was all over. I can't believe we missed that ship. I saw everything. I couldn't get to sleep. Then I heard the engine rev up and felt the boat turning right, so I jumped up and went outside to look around. All I could see was the bow of this huge ship coming at us. I started screaming we're gonna crash. A bunch of us were on deck freaking out when we barely missed the ship."

Red Sky Morning

Jesus said, "I started praying, because I thought we were going to die."

"Who was on watch?" asked Carlos.

I said, "I was. God, I'm sorry, guys. I did the best I could."

"You did better than you think." said the captain. "Remember, I was right next to you. It took a lot of courage to hang in there like you did, and there's nothing to be sorry about. You saved us and the boat."

Everyone expressed their gratitude, and Carlos walked over to me and said "My shift starts in a half-hour, but I think you've had enough for one night, so I will relieve you now."

"Thanks, because I'm exhausted. I think I'll go down to the galley and get something to eat, then try to get some sleep." By the time I got to the galley, I wasn't sure if I wanted to eat or throw up. I decided on a bowl of ice cream, dished out some Neapolitan, sat down, and tried to relax. I wondered if I did really do everything I could? Did I make the right decisions? Or was I negligent and totally fucked up, and just lucky that we didn't crash?

When you're on watch, everyone is relying on you for their safety, to avoid any danger and to alert the crew if necessary. Before this incident, I don't think I knew what responsibility really meant.

I finished my bowl of ice cream, cleaned up, and headed for my bunk. I knew I wouldn't be able to sleep, but it felt good to lie down and relax.

I opened my eyes; I could see daylight through the curtains. I looked around our quarters and there wasn't anybody in bed. I jumped out of my bunk, put my shorts and tennis shoes on, then went out on deck. The boat was running, but I didn't see anyone. I became a little disoriented and couldn't figure out what the hell was going on. I went back to my bunk and got my watch. It was nine in the morning. I guess I must have fallen asleep, but where was everybody, and why didn't someone wake me up? I ran back outside, and I could see the guys working. Where were they a second ago?

A familiar voice from behind me said, "Good morning."

"Hi, Dad, what's going on? Why didn't someone wake me up?"

"You had a pretty stressful night, so we decided to let you sleep in."

"Thanks, I guess I needed it."

He smiled and said, "You better get something to eat, and get to work. Were getting close to the fishing area."

I went back to my quarters, brushed my teeth, shaved, then headed for the galley. John was already working on lunch, but had saved me some ham and potatoes.

"How you doing? You hungry?"

"Yeah, I'm starved."

"You want me to cook some eggs? Sure you do. I make some toast too."

"Thanks, John. You're the greatest."

Over the past two months, John and I had become good friends. I liked to cook, and John was happy to show me his recipes. When fishing was slow, I helped him cook. It was not only a lot of fun, but it made the time go by faster. John had worked for my dad for a long time, and I'm sure their relationship had some impact on my relationship with John. Anyway, he was always there for me, and I enjoyed his company.

I was about halfway through my breakfast when I heard the engines rev up. I knew what that meant, so I shoveled down the rest of my meal and walked out on deck. Everyone was starting to move into position to make a set, so I responded as well.

Red Sky Morning

Mola Mola!" A term every fisherman wants to hear, because it meant a chance for more fish, more money, and closer to the time when we would go home. At least you hope that's the direction you're headed. But good old Murphy's Law can set in, and in this case it did, because this set and the next three that day were all fishless.

Casey said, "We didn't catch one fucking fish all day. This sucks."

"I told you we could have days like this. In fact, we could go for days without catching, or even seeing, any tuna at all."

He looked at me with a sad face and said, "Shit, this is a lot of work for nothing."

"Quit your crying; remember that one set where we caught 180 tons?"

"Yeah, I guess it's all part of the job. I'll tell you, I've gained a lot of respect for fisherman since I've been out here."

Chapter 14

Three days went by, and we didn't see a fish. The rest of the fleet was experiencing the same futility. We were close to New York Harbor, and the captains decided to anchor off of Ambrose Light. Within a couple of hours, most of the fleet had reached the area, and had dropped the hook. A lot of the crews knew each other and decided that while at anchor they would visit each other via the speedboats. One of the boats announced that they were going to show some porno movies that night, and all were invited.

For the last few days most of us were a little depressed, and this rendezvous with the fleet lifted everyone's sprits. John decided to have a barbecue that night. We had a mixed grill of steaks, pork, lamb chops, corn on the cob, salad Greek-style, and lots of garlic bread and homemade Dago Red. Many of the Croatians and Italian—old timers—made their own wine, which was known as, Dago Red. It was made from a mix of Grenache and Zinfandel grapes. The wine was dark in color, and had a real kick to it.

The skipper and some of the crew of the *Western King,*

joined us for dinner, and we all were having a good time. After dinner, a lot of us went over to the *Chicken of the Sea*, to watch some skin flicks. The films were vintage 1940s and were more comical than pornographic. Everyone had a good time, and by ten o'clock we all headed back to our boats.

We got back just in time for my watch. We decided to shorten the shifts to two hours, with mine running from ten to midnight. I was pretty buzzed from all the wine I drank, and if we were underway I'd have asked someone else to take my place. But we were at anchor, in about twenty fathoms of water, and the weather was calm. *Nothing's going to happen here, so the hell with it.*

It was close to midnight, and I could hardly keep my eyes open, so I went out on deck and walked around. I went down to the galley to get a glass of water, but ended up with a Coke. I was going up to the bridge when I noticed the lights of a ship headed out of New York Harbor. It looked like a cruise ship because of its size and all the lights. I knew we were not in its way, because we were anchored in a designated area. It was a clear night, and the ship lit up the sky. As it got closer, I knew it was the largest cruise ship I'd ever seen, and it was moving.

I figured it was traveling in excess of thirty knots and would pass us at a safe distance of a quarter of a mile or more.

I looked at my watch; my shift was over. I started towards the stairs, and just as I reached for the railing I saw Doug starting up the stairs. He looked up and said, "Hey, what's happening?"

"Not much, it's been pretty quiet, except for that cruise ship passing by." I pointed towards the ship. Something big and dark was between us and the ship, and it was coming straight at us. "What the hell is that?" I answered my own question." It's a wave, a fucking big wave. Hang on."

A second later, the wave crashed into our port side, and damned near washed over the whole boat. It felt like we were going to capsize, then the boat rode itself upright. Just as we got level, another wave hit us, and it was bigger than the first. It caught me off guard, and I slipped and fell to the deck. I was getting up, when I saw my dad.

"Jesus Christ, what the hell is going on?"

"The waves must have come from that cruise ship passing by. They were huge. I thought they were going to capsize us."

"It would be pretty tough to do that, but it knocked me out of my bunk. You better go down and see if everybody's OK."

Doug and I both ran down to the crew quarters to check them out. Everybody was out of their bunks, but a couple of guys were lying on the deck. The assistant engineer was out cold, and Jesus was holding his side. Carlos was kneeling next to him.

"Is he OK?" I asked.

"I think he broke a rib. What the hell hit us?"

"The wake of a huge cruise ship that went by. The wave went over our portside."

Casey said, "Must have been a big fucking ship to make a wake that big. I wonder how the other boats took it."

"I don't know, but I've gotta get back to the bridge and report to my dad.

"How's everybody down there?" asked the captain.

"Everybody seems OK, except the assistant engineer. Carlos thinks he might have a broken rib. How did the other boats take it?"

"Most of them had the same problems we're having. The crew was thrown out of their bunks, their galleys full of broken dishes, gear scattered around their decks."

"The *Pacific's* skiff slid off the net and partially sunk, but fortunately the skiff's cable was attached to their winch, or it would be lying on the bottom. You can see the crew trying to pull the skiff up, with their boom and its winches. Its going to take them some time to upright the skiff. You know they're damn heavy."

My dad got on the radio and contacted the Coast Guard to try to find out what ship had caused this. The ship was the largest passenger ship built, the United States, and it was going over thirty knots when it passed by. My father made a formal complaint, and the officer on duty said they would look into it, and let us know what action might be taken.

I watched my dad while he radioed the fishing boats to see if they needed any help. It seemed like everybody had it under control. I knew this incident troubled him, but there was something else that was bothering him.

"Well, there are a couple of things. I'm a little disappointed with the lack of fish in the area. Our plan to fish the East Coast was a poor decision. Yesterday, I found out that the balance of the fleet that stayed on the Pacific side are all on their second trip. This means big profits to them, and losses to your old man."

He lit another cigar, then continued, "The other problem is the weather. Another hurricane, much bigger than the last one, was headed for the Gulf, but now it's turning up the East Coast and headed for the Carolinas. If it hits there or further north, the swells will be much larger than the ones you saw that were generated from the last storm."

"Well, we fished in those conditions, so couldn't we still fish if the swells were bigger?"

"Well, the hurricane isn't the only problem. There's a big storm front building up in Canada and moving down this way. If that storm collides with those huge swells, you

Red Sky Morning

better hope we're in a protected harbor. Even a large ship would be at risk in that type of storm. If this happens, we could be in port for some time, and we need over 300 tons of tuna to load up. It will be a few days before the northerly storm reaches this area, if it does at all, and the same goes for those big swells. We're just pissing away the time, so go tell everyone that we're pulling up anchor. The hell with the rest of the fleet. Let's go fishing."

The crew was ready to go, and in fifteen minutes we were underway. I stayed up on the bridge so I could talk to my dad. He had been a commercial fisherman all his life and a captain for over twenty-five years. His credentials, including a Master's License, allowed him to run a ship of any size, anywhere in the world. I had gained a lot of respect for my father since we left California, and this was the first time I really felt close to him, like friends—buddies. I don't know, but it felt good, and I wanted more.

Before this trip, we had spent little real time together. Either he was gone fishing, or when he was home between trips, he was busy with the boat and cannery business. When he had any free time, he spent it with our whole family, and whatever precious moments were left, I'm sure he privately spent with Mom.

As the *Ace* moved farther out into the open sea, the swells became noticeably larger. I asked my dad if there was anything to worry about.

"Not at this time. The weather report said that the storm in Canada has stalled and may be weakening. As long as we don't encounter any heavy winds, these big ground swells won't be a problem. Anyway, were not going too far, maybe thirty to forty miles, and I plan to head toward the Cape Cod area. Last year, some boats caught a lot of tuna around that area. If there is any change in the weather we'll head for port, which would be no more that four to five hours running time."

"*Western Ace*, this is the *North Queen*, do you read?"

My dad said, "Take the wheel so I can get on the radio." I maintained course while the two captains talked. From what I could gather, three of the boats had decided to move out and continue fishing. The skipper of the *North Queen* asked my dad what his plan was. Dad relayed his plan to go farther north and to stay fairly close to shore in case the weather turned. The skipper of the *Queen* agreed, and the captains of the *Western King*, and the *Chicken of the Sea* cut in on the radio, agreeing to the plan.

I listened to them talking about how nasty the weather could get on the northeastern coast. I knew that these guys were veterans, and would not jeopardize their crews or boats, so I said to myself, there's nothing to worry about, so just concentrate on steering the boat.

Chapter 15

Dad took the wheel and I went over to look at the navigational charts. I spotted a magazine on the shelf and picked it up. It was an issue of the Pacific Fisherman. I thumbed through it, looking at the pictures. The next page showed a large purse seiner with a huge wave going over its bow. The title of the article was, *The most dangerous profession —Commercial fishing—*
I sat on the stool and started reading.

* * *

A fisherman's life is a perilous way to make a living. The U.S. Bureau of Labor Statistics has rated fishing as the most dangerous profession, with more fatalities per 100,000 workers than any other occupation. For example, mining has a fatality rate of 55 per 100,000, fishing has 140.
The Grim Reaper has always stalked fisherman at sea. During the 19th century fishing villages on the New England coast have lost as many as one hundred lives in one night, when a big storm hit unexpectedly. Since then, many im-

provements in designing boats, rigging, and electronics, especially innovations in navigation, and communication, have helped fishermen avoid major storms. Death can still come many ways. Fishermen can be swept off the deck by a big wave, or get hit by some of the rigging. Boats could go down by hitting a log, or run into the rocks while traveling in the fog, or run into another vessel. One avoidable risk is driven by greed. You could lose your boat by staying out too long, ignoring weather reports, or catching more than the capacity of your boat. A captain may violate all three of these risks, which could result in a disaster.

* * *

Shit, here we are, fishing off the New England coast with a big storm heading this way. Nah, there's nothing to worry about.

My dad spent most of his life on the sea, fishing California, Mexican, Central, and South American coasts. During this trip and at home, I heard of all the risks, fatalities, and injuries that happened while at sea. I developed a tremendous respect for the ocean, the weather, and the men who ventured into this life. It was rough and dangerous work, and being exposed to the weather and the sun made a man appear older than his age. They chose this way of life, though I saw it in their eyes—fisherman's eyes— always searching, with a gleam of optimism, determination, and a few more wrinkles than normal. They like what they do, facing a new challenge every day, unlike most nine-to-five jobs.

"Hey, son, would you take the wheel for a while so I can chart our course?"

"Sure, it gives me something to do. Should I be looking for fish?"

"A little early, but you never know. I'll be in my cabin."

Red Sky Morning

I was really enjoying the morning, just steering the boat and watching the sea. I had been at the helm for more than two hours when Casey and John came into the pilothouse.

"How's it going?" Casey asked.

"It's going great. The weather is nice and calm"

"Yeah, except for those big-ass swells. How big do you think they really are?"

"It's hard to tell because they're so far apart. Maybe thirty feet or so."

Just as we reached the crest of a slow rolling wave, I saw something on the horizon. At least I thought I saw some activity. I saw it again.

"Hey look over there. Is that fish jumping?"

John yelled, "Yeah! I also see some birds working over them." I turned the boat towards the action and pushed the throttle forward.

My dad came in. "What's going on?"

"We spotted some fish."

The crew responded immediately, getting everything ready. Frank took the wheel, and my dad headed for the crow's nest. I decided to keep Frank company, so I could watch us making a set from another vantage point and maybe gain some experience. I knew I had other responsibilities, so I intended to watch as long as I could, then head for the speedboat. As we got closer, I could see the fish boiling and jumping.

"What do you think?" I asked Frank.

"Looks like a pretty big school. Jesus, it's not only a big school, but they're bluefin tuna."

My dad's voice blared out over the intercom, from the crow's nest to the pilothouse, "Hey, Frank, do you copy?"

"Yeah, I copy. Looks like a good size school of fish."

"Best I've seen since we started working this coast."

They continued talking, with the captain giving directions

to Frank to maneuver the *Ace* into position. Frank yelled, "Looks good."

My dad whispered as if he would scare the tuna. "Slow down a little, turn ten degrees starboard, steady, steady," then he yelled, "Mola Mola! Full speed."

Frank pushed the throttle forward, and the bridge shuddered as the big diesel turned the prop. My heart was racing, this was so exciting. Frank started to turn the *Ace*, circling the school of tuna. This was serious business, and I could feel the tension as Frank concentrated on his task. I asked, "How does it look?"

Without looking at me, he said, "Looks good. Get to your post."

That's all I needed to hear. I didn't belong up here, and I quickly got down to the main deck and to my job.

It wasn't long before I was in the speedboat hauling ass, lighting seal controls, and moving back and forth between the opening in the net. I could see the tuna jumping and boiling. The skiff and the *Ace* were closing the gap, and everything looked good. Before I left my post, I took one last look at the school of fish. They were gone! Nothing boiling or jumping, like there was nothing ever there. *Shit, they must have sounded and swum out, before the purse was completely closed. On the other hand, the fish are still there, so I better get my ass in gear.*

When I got back on deck things were really moving. I took my position, and we started stacking the net. We were about half-way through when the captain joined us on the deck. He had a big grin and his eyes were gleaming. "Won't be long before we're brailing tuna. Carlos, keep an eye on the skiff. We don't want to bunch up too tight, because it looks like we got lucky."

"Hey, skipper, how much, you think?" asked Carlos.

"Over a hundred tons, for sure."

The whole atmosphere changed when we heard how big the catch was. The excitement level went up a few notches, and the whole crew started talking at once. It was why these men worked so hard, took risks, and made sacrifices, like being away from home for months at a time. It was their reward, their income, and their life. The life of a fisherman.

As we pursed up the net, the tuna were forced upward until they broke surface. The net was tightening, and there was still an open circle over 150 feet. That meant a lot of fish were in that net.

There was no way to bunch up the net one time because of the quantity of fish, so we bunched up part of the net and tuna and began to brail the fish aboard. When that section of the net was empty, we stacked it, bunched up another section, and kept going.

The sun was starting to set when we finally finished.

"How you doing son?"

"Hey, Dad. I'm a little tired, but who cares? Isn't this, what it's all about? How many tons do you think we caught?"

"More than I thought, maybe 150. Not bad for a day's work."

"Maybe we'll get lucky and find more tomorrow."

Tomorrow came and went, and we saw nothing, no birds, porpoise, and no tuna. The following morning started the same way, then around eleven in the morning we spotted a school of fish. "Mola Mola!" yelled the captain.

"God, I hope we get lots fish," yelled Casey.

"Maybe we'll load up and head in."

I shouldn't have been so optimistic. In fact, I hoped my comment didn't put the kibosh on this set, because the fish dove down under the net before we pursed up, and we got skunked.

The rest of the day proved to be unproductive. The best thing that happened was that John prepared a prime rib roast with all the trimmings. That and a few glasses of wine put me back into good spirits.

I lit up a cigarette and joined some of the crew on deck. Chi Chi saw me coming and said, "Hey, Andy, we were just talking about you."

"What about?"

"We know you have to go back to school, so when we get back in port, you be going home?"

"You know, I really haven't thought about that, but I guess I'll have to be leaving pretty soon."

"We going to miss you," said Carlos.

"You guys have been good friends, and I'll always remember the fun we had together."

We reminisced about the past two months together, then I decided to visit my dad, so I excused myself and headed for the bridge.

Jesus was at the helm, and I asked him if he had seen the captain.

"The captain just left the bridge and went to his room."

"Thanks. I follow you on watch, so I'll be back to take over."

I knocked on the cabin door and walked in. My dad was sitting at his desk; he looked up smiling. "Hi, son"

"Hey, Dad, I was just talking to the guys, and they reminded me that I'll have to be going home pretty soon, so I thought we should talk about that."

"Funny you should bring that up. I was just thinking about the same thing."

"When will we be going back to port?"

"I've been monitoring the weather, and that northerly storm has picked up some steam. It's slowly headed our way, so I don't plan to stay out here for more than a day or two. Then we'll head to Boston, where I plan to meet with John Sorenson, the president of a cannery there. That might be a good time to make arrangements for you to go back."

"How long do you plan to stay in port?"

"Probably a few days"

"Boston would be a great final port of call, with all its history and sights to see. I'm glad I'll have some time there."

We talked for a while, then I noticed that it was ten minutes to eight, so I said good night and went to relieve Jesus.

"How's it going? I'll take over now."

"OK, I see you in the morning. Good night."

There wasn't much to do, because we were not under way, but drifting. I had to be vigilant for any other vessels moving in our area. Except for the huge ground swells, the weather was beautiful. I walked out on the open deck to take it all in. It was perfectly clear, and the sun was setting in the west, a harvest moon rising in the east. It was warm and balmy, so I lit a cigarette and watched the day turn into night.

Around eight-thirty, my dad joined me on the bridge. "I decided to make a move; maybe twenty-five miles from here, so put it in gear, and we'll set a new course."

Dad kept me company for a while, then yawned and said. "We're only going three knots, so we won't reach my coordinates until six in the morning. I'm pooped, so I'll see you then. Tell the next person on watch what my plan is and to pass it on. Good night, son."

"Good night, Dad. Hope we catch some fish tomorrow."

"Yeah, me too."

Casey walked in. "Your time's up. How's it going?"

"Good. My dad decided to make a move. We're running at three knots and should arrive around 6:00 A.M. Be sure to pass that on to the next guy on watch."

"Maybe we'll get lucky."

"I hope so. See you in the morning."

Chapter 16

We were in the galley having breakfast when the speaker came to life. "We see some fish. Get ready."

"Best thing I've heard in two days," said Carlos. "Mola Mola!" We were off and running. Everything went smoothly, and our first set in almost three days, produced around twenty tons of tuna.

Everybody was pumped up, and we started looking for more fish. A few hours went by, but no more signs of fish. By lunchtime, the excitement had all but worn off. I could see it in the crew's faces. Chi Chi got up from the table and said, "I'm going to relieve the skipper up in the crow's nest, so he can have lunch."

Dad came into the galley and sat down, then helped himself to some roast chicken, mashed potatoes and gravy, and some vegetables. He poured a glass of wine and said, "Well, guys, sorry there's no fish. I thought after this morning we might run into some more."

"It's not your fault. Maybe we get lucky later," said Jesus.

For the next fifteen minutes, nobody talked, in fact, it was so quiet you could hear a pin drop.

"FISH FISH," came blaring out of the galley's speaker. It was Chi Chi, and he sounded really excited. We all jumped up and headed for the door. I heard the big diesel come to life, and the *Ace* began turning to port. The captain was already going up the stairs to the bridge, and I decided to go after him.

Frank was at the helm, and Dad was outside looking through the binoculars. I could see a lot of seagulls working an area about a mile away. Dad was on the internal phone with Chi Chi, "Looks like a big school. I'll be right up. Frank, the fish are moving westerly. Come up behind the school, and I'll call from the crow's nest."

I knew it was time for me get to my job, so I left the bridge. I ran into Chi Chi. "What do you think? Is it a big school?"

"Si, is big. Fish as far as you can see."

Chi Chi ran over to Carlos and was rattling in Spanish, then Carlos yelled, "OK, get ready!"

It seemed like an hour went by, but it was only a few minutes before we heard, "Mola Mola!"

We all knew the drill and went into action. I was in the speedboat hauling ass to the opening of the net. Chi Chi wasn't kidding; there were tuna inside the net and outside as well. I went through a box of seal controls while I worked the boat back and forth until they were together, then headed for the starboard side of the *Ace*. I hooked up the davits cables and jumped on deck, then I secured the speed boat and got ready to stack the net.

We pursed up, got the rings on deck, and tied them off. The next thing was to get one end of the net through the power block. Carlos lowered the main boom, and we pulled one end of the net through. Carlos raised the boom and posi-

Red Sky Morning

tioned it then he climbed to the second deck, where the controls were located for the power block. He turned on the power, and the net started to feed toward the deck. We just started to stack the net, and then there was a loud noise like a big THUNK, and the power block stopped.

"Ah, shit," said Carlos.

Dad was at the rail, yelling down to the main deck, "What the hell happened?"

"I don't know. Maybe the hydraulic pump blew."

"Go find Kenny and get him up here."

I ran to the engine room and got Kenny. He grabbed some tools, and we headed for the second deck. He opened up the housing. There was hydraulic fluid all over the place.

"Shit! It looks like the pump blew."

Dad was standing behind him. "You think you can fix it?"

"Not this pump. See the crack on that side."

"Don't we have a spare?"

"Yeah! The other day, I spotted a box marked, "Spare block, hydraulic pump" in the engine room."

Kenny took off, and Carlos was talking to the captain.

"What if we can't get it fixed?"

"I guess will have to bring in the net the old way."

"*Hijo-la!* It take us long time to bring in the net."

"How long do you think?"

"Maybe five, six hours."

Kenny came back, and he looked pissed off. "It looks like our previous drunk engineer scavenged a bunch of parts off the pump and never replaced them or marked the box."

"That fuckin' asshole. I knew we would eventually find something he screwed up. Well, Carlos, it looks like we'll have to do it the hard way. Let's get moving, because the last weather report said that the nor' wester is picking up speed, and headed our way. We're going to start feeling the weather in a few hours."

    Carlos got some one-inch-thick rope, around twenty feet long. He tied the two ends together to make a loop. The net was lying over the port railing. We bunched up the net as best we could, then passed one end of the loop under the net, pulled it up and through the other side of the loop. The main boom had three blocks attached to it. On top was the power block, just below that was a single block, then a double block that was used to pull up the skiff. Cables ran through these blocks and had large hooks attached to the ends. The other side of the cables would be coiled behind the hydraulic heads that were part of the winch. Carlos picked the single block. The winch man lowered the hook, and we hooked the rope around the net. The winch man took a couple of wraps around the turning head, applied some pressure by pulling on the cable, thus tightening the sling around the net. The sling and that portion of the net were lifted about thirty feet.

    The crew was positioned around the stern, and as the winch man lowered the net, the crew would stack it, laying the rings on one side of the boat and the corks on the other, with the net stacked in the middle.

    The power block would just feed the net, but now we had to pull the net down. The easiest way was to put our fingers through the mesh to get a good grip.

    It was an extremely slow process, and this net was over a mile long, which meant that we would have to raise and lower the net over one hundred and eighty times. It was tough going, but within a half-hour, we had a good rhythm going.

    Three hours later, and about half-way done, things started to change. The wind had picked up to twenty or thirty knots, and the ocean was getting choppy. Thirty-foot ground swells were rolling northerly, and the wind chop was headed south. It was getting difficult to keep balanced standing on the unevenly piled net.

Everybody was pushing themselves to the max. Our forearms and hands were screaming with pain, but this wasn't a time when you could or would take a break. Even the skipper was helping stack the net. He looked over at me and asked, "How you doing?"

"This is about as hard as I've ever worked."

"I'll second that," yelled Casey.

"It's going to take a couple more hours to stack the net, then we have a lot of fish to bring aboard. It's going to be a long night, so hang in there."

"Aye-aye, captain."

When we were almost finished stacking the net, we could see that we had so much fish in the net that we'd have to make two cuts, splitting the school into two areas, meaning we would have to bunch up twice.

By the time we were ready to brail the tuna, the wind velocity was between thirty and forty knots. The wind chop had turned into eight-foot waves, and with the opposing thirty-foot ground swells, it felt like we were in a giant washing machine.

It was starting to get scary and dangerous. We had the brailer coming up with five tons of tuna in it when the *Ace* swayed violently. We lost control of the pole, and it hit Doug square in the chest, knocking him across the deck, and slamming him into the opposite rail.

I ran over to him. He was out cold. John and I picked him up and carried him into the galley. We didn't know how bad his injures were, so we carried him to his bunk. As we laid him down, he came to. He complained about his chest hurting. I thought he might have broken some ribs, so we told him to stay put, and we got back on deck.

The captain yelled, "How's Doug?"

"He's awake, but I think he might have broken a rib

or two."

I don't know how we did it, but by 2:00 A.M., we had all the fish on board. There were ten-foot breaking waves crashing into thirty-foot ground swells, and we were in the middle of it, with one more thing to do: pull the skiff up and secure it.

Chi Chi was in the skiff, and he attached the cable to the bow plate then maneuvered the skiff behind the stern. Carlos was at the winch. He took a couple of wraps around the turning head and began to put pressure on the cable. The cable tightened up, and the skiff started to slide up the tracks, when a wave smashed into the portside, knocking the stern of the *Ace* sideways. The cable snapped, sounding as loud as a gunshot. The broken cable whipped back at all of us standing on the deck and hit Jesus across his back and right arm. Jesus went down, and was unmoving. John went to his aid, while the rest of us got another cable ready and passed it to Chi Chi.

This time we got the skiff up and secured, and the captain set a course for Boston Harbor. The ground swells were on our stern, and we were headed directly at the incoming northerly storm.

I went up to the bridge to let Dad know that Jesus was OK; the cable had just knocked the wind out of him. Other than that, he had a nasty welt across his back.

"What about Doug?"

"Well, he's up and sitting in the galley. He said his head hurt like hell, but he didn't think any of his ribs were broken."

"As soon as we get in, I'll make sure both Jesus and Doug go to the hospital to get fully checked out. God, I feel awful about this. I shouldn't have stayed out in this weather so long."

"It's not your fault the power block broke down. The way

Red Sky Morning

I see it, if that hadn't happened we would probably be in port already."

"Thanks, son, but I'm still responsible for my crew and the boat. We're still in the middle of a serious storm, and it's getting worse."

"How long before we get in?"

Maybe five, six hours. Go down and tell Carlos to make sure everything is secured, then have him come up to see me."

"Aye-aye, Captain." I saluted and took off.

Everybody was totally exhausted. Some of the crew hit their bunks, and the rest were in the galley playing cards. I tried to get some sleep, but the *Ace* was being knocked around so bad that I could hardly stay in my bunk, and sleep was impossible.

I decided to join the guys in the galley. They were playing gin rummy and needed another person to even the teams, so I joined in. An hour or so went by, and John made up some sandwiches. We hadn't eaten since lunch the day before, but until I saw food, I really didn't think much about it. Anyway, we scarfed down the first batch, and John started to make more. Suddenly, it felt like a big hand had slapped the side of the *Ace,* then another blow hit the opposite side. The *Ace* shook violently, and shit was flying in all directions. John fell on the deck, and Chi Chi fell off the end of the bench.

I helped clean up the galley, then decided to go up to the bridge. Dad was at the helm. "Everybody OK below?" he asked.

"Yeah, other than a few bruises from being knocked around. How's it going?"

"Not good. It's really hard to maintain course. The big swells lift our ass up and push us forward, then we collide with the incoming waves. It's beating the hell out of us."

"How much longer?"

"I'd say we'll lose these trailing ground swells in about two hours. After that it'll still be plenty rough, but not like this crap. These kind of conditions can break up the boat if you're not careful."

"You hungry?"

"Now that you mention it, yes. Why don't you get me something, and bring up some strong coffee. It's going to be a long night, and be careful going down."

John made up a couple of sandwiches and a pot of strong coffee. It took one hand to hang onto something, so John and I brought up the food and coffee.

"Thanks, John. How's everybody doing?"

"They're OK. This storm's a real son of bitch! Think maybe one of the worst I've been in."

"We've been through some bad ones."

"Yeah, you look tired. Want someone to take over?"

"Not now."

John left the bridge, and I kept my dad company. He wolfed down the first sandwich, then drank a couple of cups of coffee. "Man, I feel a lot better. Go to my cabin and get us some cigars."

I lit one for him, then one for myself.

There was all kind of activity on the radio. A lot of boats were in trouble, and we heard "May Day, May Day, this is the oil tanker, *Yang Yi*. We have lost power, and the situation is critical. Our position is 41.5 degrees North and 68.3 West."

"This is the U.S. Coast Guard, calling the *Yang Yi*."

"I told you that even a big ship could have problems in this kind of weather." said Dad.

"Well, we seem to be hangin' in there"

"She was designed to take on rough weather, and with all of her wells full of fish and brine water, we're sitting lower in the water and riding out the storm the best we can. If we were empty and riding high, we would be bobbing around like a cork, and it would be a hell of a lot worse."

For the next couple of hours the *Ace* took a major beating. We didn't talk much but listened to the distress calls coming over the radio. Other than that, it was great just hanging on and watching my dad work his way through this storm.

"Hey, son, go find Frank for me, and tell him I want him to take over the helm. We've lost that trailing swell, and I'm beat, and Andy, thanks for keeping me company."

"Don't mention it. You know, I've learned a lot on this trip, including just how powerful and unpredictable the ocean and Mother Nature can be. I'll get Frank. See you later."

I found Frank playing gin with some of the crew. "Hey, Frank, captain wants you to take over at the helm."

"No problem, just let me finish this hand."

He picked up another card from the deck, and flipped his discard on the table. "Gin rummy. Sorry, guys, but I think I just won." He turned his attention to me. "Your dad must be exhausted, I'll grab a cup of coffee and get right up there."

I sat down and watched the guys play cards. It took about five minutes before my eyelids started getting heavy. The *Ace* was still being knocked around. It was hard to stand, and most of the crew would be sleeping if they could. If I didn't get thrown out of my bunk, I was sure I could get some sleep.

I woke up to the sound of the engine slowing down. The *Ace* wasn't pitching around anymore, which meant we were getting close to our destination.

I looked at my watch; I couldn't believe that I had slept for over four hours. I went out on deck to look around. It was the middle of August, but you couldn't tell by the weather. I knew that my time was just about up, and I'd be going home. Boston was going to be a great final port of call with all its history and sights to see.

Chapter 17

The captain slid the *Ace* alongside the dock, and the crew secured the lines. For the rest of the day we tidied up the *Ace*. I helped Kenny in the engine room, then after lunch, I helped John clean up.

Around four that afternoon, I found myself standing on the bow smoking a cigarette and looking at the Boston skyline.

The captain yelled down from the bridge, "Hey, Andy, get cleaned up. Mr. Sorenson will be at the dock to pick us up around five thirty."

I got to the bunkroom, took a shower, shaved, and put on a nice pair of slacks and a madras plaid shirt. I splashed my face with a little cologne, combed my hair, and took a quick look in the mirror. I was ready to go. I stepped out on the deck and damn near ran into my dad.

"Looks like you're ready. That must be John standing by that car." We jumped off the *Ace*, introductions were made, and we drove off.

"Well, I hope you're hungry and like lobster," said John.

"I love lobster," answered my dad.

"How about you, Andy?"

"Lobster's great, and I brought a big appetite."

"I'm glad to hear that, because I picked up some huge lobsters this morning."

Dad and John discussed the status of the fleet. All of the boats took a beating from the storm but had made it to various ports and were safe.

Dad said that most of the boats were going back to Puerto Rico to unload then head for the Pacific Coast to fish. The initial plan was to catch one load of tuna, unload in the local area, then load up the second time, head for Puerto Rico, and unload there. The fishing was not as good as expected, and the end of the season was near. Some skippers had already decided to return to Puerto Rico as soon as they loaded up the first time. John said that would help the situation, and that they would discuss this at a later time.

We were driving through a really upscale neighborhood when John turned into his driveway. "Here we are," said John. When I got out of the car, I got a good look at the house. It was a mansion. The entrance floor was marble, and there was a fancy spiral staircase going to the second floor balcony, with lots of expensive-looking art on the walls. *This guy must be loaded.*

We followed John into the den, where a boy was watching TV. "Hey, Chris, come over here and meet our guests." Chris, like any kid, wasn't much interested in meeting his parents' friends, but he got up, shook our hands, and went straight back to the tube.

A door swung open and a beautiful woman came through, smiling. "Hi, Honey." She walked right up to us. She gave her husband a kiss, turned to us, and stuck out her hand. "Hi, my name is Erica." My dad shook her hand, then introduced me. I was happy that he referred to me as his son, Andy, instead of calling me, Andy Jr., which he'd done before.

"Would you like a drink?" asked our hostess. We both ordered a VO and soda, and followed her to the bar. Not only was she beautiful, but she had a body to go with it. *John was a lucky man.* She poured us a drink, made a Scotch and water for John, and a martini for herself.

Our conversation started with Erica asking about where we lived, kids, nationality, where I went to school, did I play football etc. John was a football fan, and was thrilled to find out I might get a scholarship to USC. He went to Penn State, a rival to USC, and went on about when he went to school and how he met Erica. "By the way, where is Nicole? She knew we were having guests for dinner."

"She went to her girlfriend's house but promised to be here for dinner."

"Nicole is our daughter. I'm sure Andy and she will have some things in common. She just graduated from high school and is starting college this semester."

Man, if she looks anything like her mother, I'll definitely find something in common. The night was looking better all the time.

Erica excused herself, because she needed to get back to the kitchen. I asked, "Is there anything I can help you with?"

She looked surprised, smiled, and said, "You could help me with these giant lobsters and open up some wine for dinner." I knew John and my dad needed to discuss some business matters, which would be boring, so helping Erica sounded like fun.

The lobsters were bigger than I thought. Erica wanted to steam them, and I said, "I hope you have a big enough pot." She showed me where the pots and pans were. There were two pans about the same size. I recommended using both of them, and she agreed.

I got busy cleaning the lobsters. I started to put some water in the bottom of one of the pots, and I heard another woman's voice.

"Hi, mom."

I turned with the pot in my hands to see who was talking and just about dropped the pot. She had to be Nicole. She was just as beautiful as her mother was.

"Nicole, this is one of our dinner guests, Andy Rafkin." She smiled, and I stood there with my mouth open.

"So, my mom's already got you working."

"Actually, I volunteered."

She walked up to me and asked, "You like to cook?"

"Yeah, I think it's fun." *Come on Andy, do or say something. Just don't stand there, holding that pot.* Thank God she broke the ice.

"What'cha cooking?"

"See those huge lobsters in the sink? I'm just about ready to put them into those pots to steam them."

She smiled, licked her lips, and in a sexy voice, said, "Mmmm, I love to eat lobster."

Introductions were made, and Nicole and I went back to the kitchen. We all got to work, and about a half-hour later, dinner was served. "What type of wine would you like with dinner?" John asked.

"I'm sure whatever you pick will be fine," answered my dad.

John decided to serve a white burgundy with the appetizers and Rothschild's Bordeaux for the meal. He opened bottles, pouring the white wine, and setting the bottle of Bordeaux down to breathe. He asked Nicole to say grace.

She started by giving thanks for the fabulous dinner, her family, and the new friends they were having that evening, and that their guests would have a great time in Boston.

Nicole sat directly across from me, which made me a little nervous. I couldn't keep my eyes off her, and I was afraid that I would drop some food or spill wine on my shirt. I tried to concentrate on dinner, telling myself, don't be a pig, cut small pieces, don't rush. The more I tried, the more nervous I got. I stopped, and told myself, *come on get your shit together, this isn't like you.* I took a breath and looked up. Nicole was looking right at me. Our eyes locked, and we smiled at each other. *Man, it was starting to get hot in here.* Erica asked Nicole to give her a hand serving the rest of the food.

Phew. Thanks, mom, for saving my butt. Nicole excused herself and followed her mother into the kitchen.

The balance of the dinner went smoothly. Nicole's salad was awesome, and the lobster was cooked perfectly. I had also prepared some drawn butter, mixed with a little lemon and a touch of garlic.

I helped clear the table, while John and my dad continued discussing business. Nicole and I hit it off. We were the same age. At least she thought we were, and had a lot in common. We helped Erica for a while, then Nicole asked, "Hey, Mom, do you mind if Andy and I go to the den?"

"Of course not, and thank you both for helping me clean up."

We left the kitchen and walked through the dining room where John and my dad were sitting. John asked, "Nicole, I promised to show our guests around Boston tomorrow, but Andy and I have some things to take care of. So, could you show his son around?"

"Sure, I'd be happy to." She looked at me and smiled, then grabbed my hand. "Come on. Let's go plan the day."

"You sure it's OK with you?"

"Not only is it OK, but I would really like to spend the

day with you, show you around, and get to know you better."

All right she likes me. We went into the den, where her brother was still glued to the TV. "Well this won't do. Let's go to the sun room where it's quiet."

"Sounds good to me."

The sunroom was an enclosed patio looking out to a huge back yard. There was a tennis court and a swimming pool, surrounded by a beautiful manicured lawn. I realized that this property was more like an estate, maybe five to six acres in size.

"You have a beautiful back yard"

"Thanks, you want to take a walk around?"

Before I could say anything, she grabbed my hand, and we went outside. The weather was nice, just a little chill in the air, but I was so into Nicole it could have been snowing and I wouldn't have noticed.

We sat on a bench next to the pool and talked about the plans for the next day. The more time I spent with her, the more I liked her. Eventually, we started talking about school, her friends, my friends, and surfing, which really interested her. We talked and laughed for more than an hour. Then she took on a serious-type look, smiled, put her arms around my neck, and kissed me full-on with her mouth open. I wasn't expecting this, but I was loving every moment. It started to get a little heavy, and we were both getting into it when she pushed back gently and stared into my eyes. She smiled and said, "Maybe we should go back to the house."

We walked back to the sunroom, and talked a little more about the next day. The plan was that she would pick me up at the boat at eight, go to breakfast, then tour the city.

The door opened. "Oh, there you are. Having a nice time?"

"Hi, Mom. Yeah we're having a great time planning what we're going to do tomorrow."

"Dad mentioned that you were going to show Andy around. Well, they're just about ready to call it a night, so wrap it up and I'll see you in the living room."

"OK, we'll be right there."

I stood up and said, "I guess we better get going."

She looked up at me and smiled. "I had a really nice time this evening"

"So did I."

I held out my hand, and she grabbed it. I pulled her up off the couch and pulled her to me, then kissed her gently. "I'm really looking forward to being with you tomorrow."

"And me, with you."

Chapter 18

When we got back to the *Ace,* I said good night to my father, lit a cigarette, and strolled to the bow. Most of the crew were in their bunks, and the deck was empty. I leaned on the railing, and looked out on the bay. The reflection of the moon shimmered across the water, and I thought of Nicole, knowing I would only be with her for a couple of days. Man, I wished she lived near me.

I woke up around three in the morning, and there was no way I was going to go back to sleep. All I could think about was Nicole and how this day would end. I drifted off, daydreaming about making love to her, and surprisingly I fell back to sleep. I woke up and it was light outside. *Oh shit, I hope I didn't screw up.* I grabbed my watch; it was 7:30. I got up, took a shower, shaved, and brushed my teeth. Nicole said to wear casual clothes, so I put on a good pair of shorts and a plaid shirt. I slipped on some tennis shoes, and went to the galley for a cup of Java.

It was around 8:20 when Nicole pulled up in her red Porsche. *Wow, what a car!* I realized that I had never asked her what kind of car she had. Well, was I impressed, and so were the other guys. They were whistling and giving me a bad time as I walked down the ramp. I was sure Nicole could hear them; how embarrassing. She got out of the Porsche and posed for a moment. It suddenly got quiet. She looked out of sight. She wore a skintight sweater, and a really short pleated skirt that showed off her beautiful legs and her above-average boobs. She was enjoying the whole thing; I think she was posing deliberately. She ran up to me, gave me a big hug, then kissed me passionately. It got even quieter. I looked up at the crew, whose mouths were hanging open, waved and walked to her car.

"You want to drive?"

"I'd love to."

"The keys are in it."

I went around and opened the door for Nicole, who slid right in. As I slipped into the driver's seat, I looked up at my fellow crewmembers still standing there in a stupor. I turned the ignition key, and the Porsche's powerful engine came to life. I revved it up a couple of times, waved at my friends, and took off.

"Well, do you think I impressed your friends?"

"You mean looking sexy, and hugging and kissing wasn't just for me?"

"Of course it was, but I still wanted to look good."

"Well, don't worry; you definitely left a lasting impression on those guys. So, where are we headed?"

"I thought we would start with a light breakfast at my favorite diner, then tour the city.

The day flew by, and Nicole invited me to a party that night. She dropped me off at the *Ace* around four and planned to pick me up at eight.

The second my foot hit the deck, I heard the whistles from the guys

"Hey Andy, how was it?"

"She's out of sight, did you get any?"

They kept razzing me, but I just smiled at them and went down to the galley. That was a mistake, because the rest of the crew was sitting there, and they all gave me more shit. Again I just smiled and said nothing, which pissed them off because they wanted to hear something juicy.

I finally went up to the bridge for some peace and quiet, and ran into my dad.

"How did the day go?"

"It was fantastic! Nicole is a really neat girl. If she lived in San Pedro or close by, she'd be my choice to go steady with."

"I'm glad you're having a good time. Speaking about San Pedro, I need to make plans for you to go back."

"Where would I fly out of?"

"Probably New York because, the rates are much cheaper. We would only need to set up transportation from here to there."

"Well, that might not be too hard, because Nicole is planning to drive down to her college a couple of weeks early to visit her new sorority and get ready to start school."

"Don't you think that might be out of line?"

"I don't think so. Anyway, were going out tonight, so I'll ask her."

"Well, let me know, so I can make reservations".

"I'll tell you tomorrow morning. I can't believe how fast this summer went by. I've had such a good time, and it's been really great to spend this time with you."

He gave me a big hug, then gripped my shoulders; he had tears in his eyes. "God, I've missed watching you grow up, so I can't tell you how important this time together is to me."

Now both of us had tears rolling down our cheeks.

We hugged for a long time, then I heard the dinner bell.

"Ah, dinner time, I'm starved. You coming?"

"I've got to review some paperwork, so I'll see you in the galley in a few minutes. Save me a seat."

John must have been in one of his creative culinary moods, because dinner was fantastic. First he served a lobster salad with vinaigrette dressing and fresh baked bread, followed by a bowl of French onion soup that made our tastebuds come alive. For the main course, he had barbecued a few racks of lamb on the rare side, then covered them with Dijon mustard, sprinkled them with mustard seeds and rosemary, and zapped them under the broiler. With the lamb, he served garlic-mashed potatoes, and string beans.

With every mouthwatering bite and sip of Dago red, dinner just got better and better. I ate way too much; in fact, the whole crew pigged out. There wasn't a bite of food on anyone's plate, or on any serving platter. We all complimented John, then let him rest while we cleaned up.

After we finished cleaning, a few of us went out on the deck to have a smoke. I told my friends that I was going home, and that I would be leaving in a day or two. They were disappointed that I was leaving but understood. I looked at my watch and it was seven-thirty.

"Shit. I've got to get ready for my date. See you guys later."

I got ready in fifteen minutes and was on the dock ten minutes early. Eight o'clock came and went. It was eight fifteen, and I was starting to get worried. *Shit maybe she stood me up. What a bummer.* I lit a cigarette, and started to pace back and forth. Casey yelled down, "Looks like you got stood up," There were a few chuckles from the group. *Man, am I glad I'm leaving soon, because these guys will never let me live this down.*

It was eight twenty-five, and I started to head for the

gangway when the red Porsche came flying around the corner. It came to a screeching halt, and Nicole jumped out and ran up to me. "God, I'm really sorry for being so late, I got a call from the president of my sorority and had to make plans for moving in. I had to talk with my parents and make a few calls. I hope you're not mad?"

"No way, I'm just glad you're here".

"So am I"

She put her arms around my neck, kissed me, and said, "Ready to party?"

"Absolutely"

"Why don't you drive?"

I opened the passenger door, Nicole slid in, and I looked up on the deck where the boys were watching and gave them a little wave. There were a few whistles and remarks, so I just looked up and smiled.

It took twenty minutes to get to Nicole's friend's house. The party was rockin'. Nicole introduced me to Brent, who was throwing the party.

"I hear you're from California?"

"Yeah, I live on the coast in Los Angeles".

"I'm going to UCLA this semester, in fact that's why I'm having the party. Ill be leaving in a few days. Be sure you give me your phone number. Nicole told me you're a surfer. Maybe you could teach me"

"Sure, that would be fun."

"There's a keg of beer in the kitchen. Help yourself.

Nicole grabbed my hand, and said, "Let's get a drink."

We drank, danced, and I met a lot of Nicole's friends. We walked out on the deck to get some fresh air. I told Nicole about my plans to fly home in a couple of days, via New York. Before I had a chance to ask her if I could get a ride, she said, "I decided to move into the sorority house early. I plan to leave in a couple of days so I could take you there. It'll be fun, and we could spend a little more time together."

"That's really nice of you, but I don't want to put you out. You'd have to drive farther than you need to."

"That's OK. I could go shopping in the big city before I go to school. So that's what were going to do, OK?"

"Sounds great to me. I'll start packing tomorrow morning."

It was getting late. And most of the people had left the party. I realized that we were the only people in the living room. Nicole couldn't stop talking about our little tour of the East Coast. She was about two-thirds of the way through planning our itinerary when I had this big urge to kiss her. I put my arm around her and pulled her close while she was rattling away. She stopped talking and stared into my eyes. I kissed her passionately.

Our faces were an inch apart, and I said, "If we leave tomorrow, where are we going to spend the night?"

She smiled and whispered, "I guess we'll have to get a hotel room."

"I've never rented a room before."

She smiled, wrapped her arms around me, and whispered, "Neither have I, but I can't think of anyone I'd rather be with."

"It's getting late, and tomorrow is going to be a big day, so maybe we should go."

"Yeah, I think you're right. I have to figure out what I'm going to tell my parents."

"Think you'll have any problems?"

"I don't think so. I'll tell them that we're driving directly to the college, and you're going to stay at the Kappa Beta Phi frat house."

"That sounds believable. I'll tell my dad the same story, just in case he talks to your dad about this."

Red Sky Morning

I was a little buzzed from the beer, so I asked Nicole to drive. We got back to the *Ace,* and she stopped and turned off the ignition. That signaled that she wanted to stay a while, and I was all for that. In one second, we were all over each other. I didn't realize how small a Porsche was until then.

Nicole was fairly tall, and being six-three and two hundred and forty pounds made it difficult. Nicole was on top of me, and she reached down to push the lever to drop the seat back. It fell back so fast, I slid sideways and got stuck between the two bucket seats. I was in pain, but laughing. Nicole's arms were around me, and she was stuck as well. We both started cracking up. The harder we tried to get unraveled, the harder we laughed. We stopped for a moment, then started making out again. Whatever pain I felt before, was now gone.

Nicole said, "we'll have plenty of time for this tomorrow, so let's get free before one of your crewmates see us".

"Shit, I didn't think of that."

When we really tried, it didn't take long to get back up to our seats. Nicole was straightening out her hair, and I sat there looking at her. She looked gorgeous. *You lucky shit, you get to spend two nights with her.*

"What time do you think we'll leave tomorrow?"

"I'm going to tell my parents that I want to leave as early as possible so we can get to my school."

"Around what time?"

"Let's try for one o'clock. You have my number, so call me around nine, and I'll know by then."

We hugged and kissed, then said good-by. I stood there watching the Porsche take off. I pulled out a cigarette and my Zippo, lit up, and took a big draw. I blew the smoke straight up in the air, turned and headed for the gangway. Man, was I pumped up.

Chapter 19

I was up at 6:00 A.M. and started packing. I didn't have a lot of clothes, so it didn't take long to get ready. I put my bags on my bunk and went to the galley. John was at the sink getting stuff ready for breakfast.

"Good morning"

John turned and smiled. "Good morning to you. I heard you're going to leave us."

"Yeah, in fact I'm leaving today. That's why I came down here early, I wanted to say good-bye, and thank you for everything. Working with you in the kitchen was a lot of fun and made me feel at home."

John's eyes watered a little, and he hugged me. "We had a good time together, no?"

"Yeah, we sure did. I'll miss you. Don't kill anybody with that cleaver." We laughed.

"You have a safe trip back." John turned and got back to work.

It was time to talk to the captain. When I got to the bridge, I found my dad reviewing some charts.

"Hi, son, how's it going?"

"Going good. I talked to Nicole about having her take me to New York."

"What did she think about it?"

"She was all for it. In fact, she sort of volunteered. We plan to leave today."

"I don't think I can make arrangements that quick."

"You don't have to. We plan to drive to her sorority and she's making arrangements for me to spend the night at a nearby fraternity. We'll spend the next day there, and the following morning we'll drive to New York."

"Let's see, that will be Tuesday. I'm sure we can get reservations for then. Why don't we give the airlines a call."

Dad called American Airlines and made the reservations. I was booked on the redeye, living La Guardia Airport at 11:00 P.M., Tuesday night. It was only seven-thirty, and I couldn't call Nicole yet so I walked around the deck saying goodbye to the crew, which took me a half an hour. Now, there was nothing to do but wait. I was so anxious to see Nicole and get on the road. The hotel room . . . yeah, the hotel room. I was going crazy.

I went down to the galley to get some coffee, like I really needed some caffeine. I poured a cup, grabbed a roll, and sat down. I tried not to look at my watch. Didn't work. 8:10, 8:15, 8:25. *What's come over me?* Just then, Carlos came in and said, "Hey, Andy, there's someone here looking for you."

"Who is it?"

"She's really pretty."

I jumped up so fast I felt a little dizzy. I shook it off and thanked Carlos.

"Where is she?"

"She's on the deck, by the ramp."

I ran to the starboard side. There she was, in her skintight jeans and sweater. She looked awesome.

"Hi."

"Hi back."

She hugged and said, "Last time I was late, and I had no way to reach you. Today I'm early. I hope that's OK?"

"No problem, I'm ready to go. I thought we were going to leave around one."

"I know, but when I talked to my parents about going, they were concerned about us leaving too late, driving at night, and getting to my sorority house too late. So, here I am."

"I'll get my bags."

"Not so quick. Since I'm early, why don't you show me around the boat and introduce me to your friends."

"OK, let's start with the bridge. My dad's quarters are up there, and I need to say good-bye."

I knocked on my dad's door. "Come in."

"I knocked because Nicole is with me"

"I'm dressed, come on in."

We said our goodbyes, and Dad handed me a wad of money. "Here's a little advance on your pay."

"Thanks, I can use it." *If he only knew.*

I gave him a hug and said, "Thanks for letting me come fishing with you this summer. It's been a great experience that I'll never forget."

"Well fishing is a tough way to make a living, and as you know it's not getting better. We have to go farther, and stay out longer, to catch fish. There are more countries expanding their fishing fleets, which has increased the competition for the same fish we're after."

"Yeah, I know. Don't worry, the only type of fishing I'll be doing is sport fishing, which I love to do."

"Well, you guys better get going. It was nice to meet you Nicole and good luck at college."

"Thank you, Mr. Rafkin. Have a safe and successful trip."

We left the bridge and spent the next half-hour meeting some of the crew and touring the *Ace*.

Nicole was having fun flirting with the crew, who went gaga over her. It was fun, and definitely an ego booster for me. It was time to go, so I grabbed my bags, and we were off.

Nicole wanted to drive so I could see the sights, but the only sight I was interested in was Nicole. "So, what have you planned for us today?"

"I thought we'd take a ride up to Cape Cod. It's really nice, and because summer is almost over, it shouldn't be too crowded."

"How long will it take to get there?"

"About two and a half hours."

"Then where?"

"Oh, I thought we would spend the day messing around, then find a neat little cottage to spend the night."

We had a great day. Nicole had vacationed there before and knew what to see and where to go. We had a light lunch, then she looked at me, smiled, and said, "Maybe we should start looking for a place to spend the night."

"Yeah, maybe we should."

The first place we looked at seemed really nice. I was so nervous when I asked for a room that I wasn't sure what the hell I was saying. The manager showed us a room, which was OK, but we decided to look elsewhere. By the third hotel, neither of us felt nervous, and we both loved the room. It was a little more expensive, but it was a separate cottage with a small living room and a fireplace. It was right on the beach.

We checked in, paid for the night, then parked next to the cottage. We set our bags down inside and just looked at

Red Sky Morning

each other, kind of not knowing what to do next.

"You want to take a walk on the beach?" I said at last.

Nicole was blushing and answered, "Should we change into our bathing suits?"

"I guess we should."

We started to unpack, then we stood there for a moment. Nicole made the first move. She pulled her sweater over her head, then unbuttoned her jeans. I stared at her, in her bra and panties. She looked at me and said, "Well, aren't you going to change?"

I had no idea why I was so nervous, but I started pulling my clothes off, got naked, and grabbed my trunks. I had one foot in and looked up at Nicole, who was standing there with no top on. I couldn't believe what happened next. I started to put my other foot in my trunks, while staring at Nicole, got off balance, and fell right on my face. She started to crack up, and then I was the one blushing. By the time I regained my composure, she had her bikini on and said, "You ready to go?"

. It was a beautiful day, the seas were calm, and the sky was clear blue, except for a few wispy clouds. We walked hand in hand along the waters edge talking about past experiences and our future plans. We must have walked for over an hour, and I had an urge to take a dip. I started to run, then turned toward the water and ran in until it was deep enough to dive.

On the beach, I saw Nicole running towards me. It was like in slow motion watching her run, laughing and her hair flowing in the breeze. She dove through a small wave and came up right in front of me. She wound her arms around my neck, pulled herself close, then kissed me passionately and said, "Maybe we should start heading back."

"Not a bad idea. I saw a liquor store about a block from our cottage." I wanted to get something to drink and snack on while we watched the sunset.

It took over an hour to get back to our cottage by the sea. Nicole went in to freshen up, and I went to the liquor store. I bought some cheese and crackers, two six-packs of Coors, and a bottle of Chandon Brut Champagne. I normally don't drink champagne, but tonight was special, and definitely called for a little bubbly.

When I got back, Nicole was watching TV. She had changed into some white shorts and a red and blue halter-top cut above her belly-button.

"What did you get? I hope you got something to eat."

"They didn't have much, but I bought some cheese and crackers, beer, and for later, a bottle of champagne."

"Umm, I love champagne, but right now cheese and crackers sounds really good."

"I see you've already taken a shower, and I definitely need one, so I'll be back in a few."

The shower felt great. I got the water as hot as I could stand and soaped up. I started to rinse the shampoo and soap off, and as I opened my eyes, the shower door clicked open. Nicole stepped in. "I was getting lonely. Want me to wash your back?"

"Uh, uh, uh, yeah, sure."

We became one, our bodies entangled. The shower was hot, but it was getting a hell of a lot hotter in there. Our animal instincts had taken control. From the shower, dripping wet, to the bed, we remained locked in the heat of passion.

* * *

Pop! The cork from the champagne bottle went flying. We were sitting on top of a sand dune, watching the sunset. I filled Nicole's glass, and saw her smiling at me. Her hair was glistening from the setting sun and rippling in the breeze.

"You look beautiful." I raised my glass. "To an unbelievable day, with an unbelievable woman."

We were frozen in time, staring into each other's eyes. Unbidden, tears began flowing from her eyes.

"What's wrong?"

"You're leaving, and as much as I want to love you and be with you, deep down I know that we'll only have this time together. I want you to know that I wish you lived near me, or that you were going to the same school. But you're not, and I want us to make the most of the time we have left."

And that's exactly what we did. Starting with dinner at the Oyster Bay, which cost me a bundle but was worth it. After dinner, we went back to our cottage. I made a roaring fire and spread a blanket in front of it. We made love and stayed in each other's arms until morning.

The next day, we were off sight-seeing and working our way towards New York.

We had a great time, as we drove down the highway listening to the radio. I was thinking about what a great time I was having, when I thought, *man, our time together is really growing short*. Now I was the one feeling bummed out. Shit, I'll never meet or be with anyone like Nicole.

"Andy, you OK?"

"Yeah, I'm all right. Just thinking of you, and how much I'm going to miss you."

Chapter 20

Nicole left early to get back to her sorority. It was only two o'clock, so I decided to stay in Manhattan and see the sights. First, I took a cab to the Empire State Building. The weather was great, and the view from the lookout level was spectacular. I took pictures as I walked around the floor. I was happy that I had bought an extra roll of film, because I used a whole roll taking pictures of Nicole. I spotted the Statue of Liberty, took a snapshot, and decided that it would be my next destination.

I took the Staten Island Ferry to Liberty Island, enjoying the skyline of Manhattan. Then I did something I'd always wanted to do, ride on a subway. I got totally lost but eventually ended up in Times Square

It was getting towards the end of the day, and the sidewalks were full of people. I was amazed at how crowded it was. I spent the next couple of hours walking around, just people watching.

I was getting hungry. I looked at my watch; it was 6:30. I decided to find a nice restaurant to have dinner, then head for La Guardia Airport. I hailed a cab and asked the driver if he could recommend a good steakhouse.

"Alfred's is the best in Manhattan. It's an old place and a bit pricey, but you get what you pay for."

"Is it far from here? "

"About a ten-minute drive. My name's Frank. You're not from here. On vacation?"

On the way to Alfred's, I told Frank about my summer's experience, and that I was leaving for L.A. tonight. Frank said business was a little slow, and he would be happy to take me to La Guardia after I finished dinner.

Old Frank was right. The food was fantastic. I ordered their thick-cut New York, baked potato, a spinach salad with bacon dressing, and a bottle of the house red wine. The salad was huge and served with garlic bread as tasty as I've ever had. When the waiter brought the main dish, the steak was at least a pound and a half, and grilled to perfection.

"Dessert?"

"No thanks, I'm stuffed. How about a cup of strong coffee and the check."

Frank said he would pick me up at eight-thirty. I checked my watch. I had fifteen minutes, so I sat back, relaxed, lit up a cigarette, and enjoyed another cup.

When I stepped outside, I saw Frank standing by his cab. He spotted me and opened the trunk. I threw in my bags, and we were off. After a few jokes and a couple of stories, Frank stopped in front of American Airlines. It was nine-thirty. I checked my bags, got my ticket, and found Gate 24.

There were only a few people waiting, but I was early. I picked up a new issue of *Surfer magazine*, took a seat, and started to thumb through it. Looking at the pictures, I realized just how much I missed California.

I thought about the summer and how lucky I'd been to experience everything. I thought about all the places I'd been and the people I'd met. A beautiful girl in every port. Unbelievable.

But one of the best things was the time I spent with my father, who, prior to this summer, I only saw a few days between fishing trips. Spending the whole summer with him gave me the opportunity to get to know him, and become friends. It was great to watch him in his domain, puffing on his cigar, while barking out orders to his crew, who had nothing but respect for him. At the end of the day, he would drink and shoot the shit with the same men, laughing and joking. He was the boss, but he was still one of the guys. I gained a tremendous amount of respect for my father, and came to understand what an awesome amount of responsibility he had being captain.Spending this time with my father had satisfied a big void in my life. That relationship and the overall experience broadened my perception and gave me a solid foundation as I entered adulthood.

"Passengers on American Airlines, Flight 1746, now loading at Gate twenty-four." I was reading an article about surfing in Australia when the page came over the speaker. It had been a little over an hour since I sat down, and when I looked around the area, it was still almost empty of passengers. When we started to board the plane, I counted only fifteen people.

With my boarding pass in hand, I stepped into the plane. There was a bitchin'-looking flight attendant directing the passengers. When it was my turn, she smiled and said, "Welcome aboard"

I locked eyes with her, handed her my boarding pass, and jokingly asked, "Any room in first class?"

She continued to smile, looked at my pass, and to my amazement, she extended her hand, turned to her right, and said, "First Class, this way."

I was stunned but followed her. I was the only person in First Class, and I didn't know what seat to take. "Looks like you've got First Class all to yourself," said the flight attendant.

"So where should I sit?"

"Wherever you like." She held out her hand and smiled. "My name is Erin, and I'll be your flight attendant this evening."

'Wow, thanks Erin."

"We had two First Class passengers scheduled for tonight, but I learned that they changed planes for an earlier flight. It's a long and boring flight with no one to talk to. When I saw you walking up the ramp, I thought there's a good-looking Californian-type guy. Be nice to have him in First Class. You surprised me when you asked me as you handed me your boarding pass. I thought, who would know? So, I directed you to First Class, and here we are."

"Flight Attendants prepare for takeoff. Good evening, everyone. My name is Ron Eshelmen, and I will be your captain this evening. We'll be taking off on time, and the weather looks good for most of the flight. There's a low pressure area over Utah, and Colorado, and it could get bumpy. The Fasten-Your-Seat-Belts sign will light up. At that time, please get to your seat and buckle up. Thank you for flying American Airlines and have a nice flight."

By now, Erin had already made me a VO and soda, and we were sitting together as the plane taxied down the tarmac. The plane slowed, made a u-turn, and stopped. I could hear the big jet engines accelerating even though we weren't moving, probably because the captain was standing on the brake. When he released, we shot forward and quickly increased speed as we rolled down the tarmac. It wasn't long before we were up and on our way.

Erin was so cool; she brought me anything I wanted. I

wasn't very hungry since I had pigged out at Alfred's a few hours earlier. I had some appetizers and a good bottle of Chardonnay. I followed her to the galley, and we talked as she made up a dish, the first chance I had to really check her out. Her face could have been from on the front page of Vogue, and she could definitely be a Playboy centerfold with that body.

She caught me checking her out, and she smiled. I think she was blushing a little.

"Well, I'm finished, so if you would bring the wine, we'll sit and munch on these goodies."

"Should I bring a glass for you?"

"I shouldn't be sitting with you or eating anything, but I'll take a chance, except for drinking. I might get in trouble sitting with you, but I would lose my job if I was caught drinking."

An hour went by, and we were having a great time. I was starting to get a buzz and decided to slow down a little. The last thing I wanted to do was get drunk and make a fool of myself.

A chime went off, and a light appeared above the cockpit door. Erin said, "The crew probably wants their dinner." She bent in close and kissed me. I couldn't help but respond. I wanted to keep going, and she didn't resist, but I knew it wasn't right. I gently pulled back and looked into her eyes. She gave me a sexy smile and said, "I'll be back; it shouldn't take long."

As I watched her walking up the aisle, I thought I must be dreaming. I'm just not this lucky.

It took Erin about fifteen minutes to serve the crew, then she was back next to me.

"See, that didn't take long." She leaned over and kissed me, then we were all over each other.

"Aren't you afraid of getting caught?"

"Not tonight. There are only a few passengers in coach, the curtains between them and us are drawn, and most of them are sleeping."

"How about the other flight attendants?"

She smiled. "After serving dinner to the crew, I called back and asked them not to bother us."

I pulled her close, and we began to get hot and heavy. My hand was under her skirt, she had unbuckled my belt, and my pants were partway down when a buzzer went off. Erin looked up. "Shit, the captain wants me." She pulled away and started to tidy up. I did the same, pulling up my pants and and my zipper. A shot of pain came from my dick, and I realized what I had done."Oh no! Does it hurt?"

"Ohhh, yeah."

"Is it bad?"

"I don't know. I'm afraid to move. Take care of the captain. I'll take of this."

Erin got on her way, and I very slowly tried to pull my zipper down. It hurt like hell, but there was no way this should ruin the night. I gritted my teeth and yanked it down. Fuck, it smarted. I felt a little dizzy, but as the pain subsided, I checked myself out. No blood, but I had a nice welt on the head of my dick.

I needed a drink, so I walked—carefully—to the galley, and took a look in the booze cart. I found a bottle of Remy V.S.O.P. and a crystal brandy glass. I poured a good two inches worth, swirled it around, and took a healthy slug. It tasted good and warm as it went down, and it seemed to take the edge off.

Erin came out of the cockpit door with the dinner trays and dishes in her hands. She entered the galley and saw me standing there.

I grimaced with pain. "Hi."

"Hi, I'm back"

She put the trays in a compartment and began to wash her hands. "How are you? I bet it hurts."

"It hurts, but I'll live."

She moved up close to me, gave me one passionate kiss, and looked straight into my eyes while she unhooked my belt. "Maybe I can kiss it and make it better."

"It's feeling a lot better. Oh man, is it feeling a lot better."

God, I wanted her. I grabbed her shoulders and pulled her up to me. Erin whispered in my ear, "I think we should join the mile-high club."

"What's that?"

"Well, we're over five miles up and . . ."

"You don't need to say anymore, but right here?"

"I don't know, maybe not a good idea.

We were at each other again. Man, she was getting hot. "How about the head?" I asked.

"Yeah, that could work."

Together, we shuffled up the aisle, opened the head door, and slipped in. It was tight but manageable. Erin pulled my shirt off, then I started taking off her clothes. We moved around trying to find the best position in the cramped space. It didn't take long before we were making love.

The plane started to shake when it hit an air pocket, and the cabin shook all over. It was unreal; all we had to do was relax and let the plane bounce around. In ten minutes, we both climaxed together. It was intense. We remained locked, holding each other as tight as we could.

I put on my clothes first with a little help from Erin and left the head to give her more room. My cognac was sitting where I left it, so I picked it up, and headed for my seat. *What an unbelievable night.*

I took a couple of sips of cognac and leaned my head

back. I must have dozed off a little, but Erin's lips on mine woke me right up. "You were, and are fantastic."

"You were awesome; I've never experienced anything like that."

"Most people never will."

We hugged and said nothing for over ten minutes, then Erin whispered, "Will we see each other after this flight?"

"If I have anything to say about it, absolutely!"

She hugged and kissed me, and whispered in my ear, "Good, because I like you, and I want to be with you. We're getting close to L.A., and I have to clean up and get ready for landing. Would you like anything?"

"How about another trip to the head? Just kidding. I'm fine, except for one thing."

"What's that?"

"Your phone number and address."

Chapter 21

Before we actually landed, Erin and I kissed and said our good-byes. I got off the plane and headed for the baggage area. My sister was picking me up, and after getting my bag, I stepped out to the street. I spotted my sister's new VW bug and waved her over to the curb. My bags barely fit in the trunk

I jumped in, and we were off. We talked about my trip, and she talked about how excited she was to start her second year at U.C.L.A. Sorority this, sorority that. I started to think about Nicole and her starting college. Man I'll never forget her or the special time we had together.

"Andy, are you listening to me?"

"Yeah, sorry. I was just thinking about seeing everyone."

We finally got home, and Mom was waiting at the door. We hugged, and said our hellos, then we all went to bed. It was around five in the morning, and I couldn't get to sleep because I was so excited to see my friends, and go surfing. I lay in bed thinking of my adventure and how lucky I had been to experience everything. I reminisced about leaving

L.A., with my dad, landing in New Orleans, flying in a hurricane. That's as far as I got before I finally drifted off to sleep.

When I woke up I felt groggy, probably jet lag. I looked at my watch. It was eleven o'clock; I couldn't believe I had slept so long. I jumped out of bed, went to the bathroom, then headed for the kitchen.

"Hi, mom."

"Good morning, you want something for breakfast?"

"Yeah, I'm starved."

"How about some eggs and toast?"

I opened the fridge, spotted some cheese and sliced ham. "You mind if I make myself an omelet?"

"So, you still like to cook?"

"I had a lot of practice on the boat."

"You know where everything is, so go ahead."

I found a bell pepper, an onion, some spinach, and mushrooms. I cut up some cheese and ham, then chopped up the veggies. I got out mom's biggest frying pan, and cooked up a huge four-egg omelet.

I polished off the omelet, four pieces of toast, and close to a quart of milk, then I cleaned up my mess, and got ready to go to the beach. I got my keys to my '34 Ford, and went to the garage.

There it was, just as I left it, a little dusty, but the thirty coats of Tahitian red lacquer shone through the dust. I couldn't wait to get behind the wheel. It was a three-window coupe with a jump seat in the rear. It had a '56 Buick engine under the hood, Bored out to the maximum cubic inches. It had an Iskenderian racing camshaft, was fuel injected, and had a Magneto ignition system. The running gear came out of a Corvette, and the clutch was custom-made. The rear tires were twelve- inch- wide racing slicks, and it had chrome rims. I still didn't know its top speed, but it was quick off the starting line and kicked ass drag racing.

Two of my neighbors, Larry and Roy, and I spent a whole year working on my hot rod. Larry had a 1929 Ford convertible, totally beefed up. It was painted canary yellow, and had a supercharged 1948 Ford engine. It had chrome rims and extra wide slick tires on the rear, and it was fast!

When we wanted to see how fast our hot rods were, we went where other owners in the area hung out. The A&W or Witch Stand Drive-ins were the spots where all the challenges and wagers were made for street drag racing. Larry and I would cruise both places, trying to pick up a race. Rarely did Larry lose.

Roy and I worked on his dad's charter fishing boat during previous summer vacations. He had a 1932 Ford coupe with a '56 Corvette engine and running gear. It wasn't as fast as Larry's, but it was in really cherry condition.

I opened the garage, slid my surfboard into the jump seat, and climbed into my rod. I put the key into the ignition and turned it to start, nothing happened! Shit, the battery was dead. I pushed the car into the street, got it rolling downhill, hopped in, put it in second gear, and popped the clutch. The big engine turned over but wouldn't start. I pumped the gas pedal a few times, popped the clutch again, and the engine came to life. It had been nearly three months since the engine had run, so I pulled over and let it warm up. After a few minutes, it was still idling rough, so I revved it up a couple of times to clean it out. That did the trick. I put it in gear and shot out on the road.

Cabrillo Beach was only a couple of miles away, and a few minutes later, I was parking my rod, downhill of course. I grabbed my board and headed for the beach. I didn't care if the waves were any good; I just wanted to get in the water.

I was surprised to see how good the waves were. There was a south swell running, and the waves were four to five feet high. As I stood there watching, I spotted a few of my friends out in the water. A couple of seconds later, I was paddling through the surf. When I got through the surfline I paddled out to where my friends were sitting on their boards. There was Duff, Stanley, Rick, Scott . . . shit, everybody was there.

My best friend, Duff, spotted me first. "Hey, Andy, when did you get back?"

"Last night. Actually it was around five this morning."

"You picked a great day. Can you believe this surf?"

"It's awesome. I hope I remember how."

"Let's get together later. I want to hear about your trip"

"Sounds good."

A nice set was rolling in, so I positioned myself to take the next wave. I started paddling and felt the swell lifting me. One more stroke and I was up and dropping down the face. It was time to make my turn, but my timing was off, and I wiped out.

It took a few rides to get back in the groove, then I spent the rest of the afternoon surfing and talking to my buddies. The tide was dropping, and the wind was starting to blow. The waves were getting blown out, and it was getting late, so most of us called it a day and paddled in. It blew almost every afternoon here. The wind came off the hills of Palos Verdes Peninsula and wrapped around Point Fermin, which caused it to howl. It was a great area to max out your sailboat. The local sailors nicknamed the area, "Hurricane Gulch."

I set my board down in the sand and stood looking at the waves, feeling the wind in my face. "You leaving?" Duff asked.

"Not yet. I think I'll stick around for a while."

"OK then, I'll see you later."

Duff took off, and I sat down on my board. While I was watching the surf, a gust of wind and a spray of sand hit me. I winced, then settled down, letting my mind wander. I saw Nicole running down the beach. Not this beach, but in Cape Cod, then I was fishing with Armando in Puerto Rico, Rosa's face, a rogue wave smashing into the *Ace*, Erin licking cream off my face, the S.S. United States steaming down on us, Ed jumping off the bow—

"Hey Andy, what's happening?"

"Uh . . . oh, hey Kathy, how's it going?"

"Sorry I startled you."

"That's OK. I was just thinking about this summer."

"I missed you. Did you have a good time?"

"It was more than just having a good time. It was truly an adventure. I saw and did more things in the last three months than I could imagine, but it is nice to be back."

Kathy LeCroix was a real surfer girl, just like the Beach Boys sang about. She was cute, had a great body, and she could surf as good as most of the guys. We were really good friends. Why our relationship didn't get serious . . . well who knows? She sat down next to me, and we talked for over an hour, until the sun started to set.

"It's getting cold, and late. I should be getting home," Kathy said.

"You need a ride?"

"Oh, I forgot to tell you. I got a car for my birthday. It's a VW van, and I love it."

We got up and hugged. She smiled, and started to walk away, then turned and yelled, "I'll see you at the game Friday night. Good luck."

When I got home, I called Jan. Her mom answered and was surprised that I was back. She said that Jan didn't say anything to her. It was then that I realized that I forgot to call her. I told her mom that it was a last-minute decision to come home. She told me that Jan was in Catalina and wouldn't be home till Monday.

    Like I thought, Jan was out having fun, and I couldn't blame her. Hell I was having such a good time I forgot to even let her know I was coming back. Maybe we were drifting apart, maybe it was time to move on. I know I'm going to date Erin. How much or how long, who knows. Later that evening, Duff stopped by, and I learned that Jan was in Catalina with John Harrington. I knew John; he played football with me and was a nice guy. Well, that settled it. Jan had John and I hopefully had Erin.

    I officially broke up with Jan and continued seeing Erin. She had a busy schedule, flying with layovers in New York, but when she was at home we were with each other. Erin and another flight attendant shared a bitchin' apartment on The Strand in Manhattan Beach. Fortunately, there were a lot of times when her roommate was laid over, and we had the apartment to ourselves. We had a fantastic relationship, even though Erin was a stone fox and a little older. I didn't feel insecure, but deep down I knew, eventually, someone older with money, nice car, respectable job, etc. would enter into her life, and our relationship would fade. Until that time, I planned to spend as much time with her as possible. Life was good.

Chapter 22

It was Friday night. The fans roared when our team ran onto the field. We were the Pirates, undefeated that season. Our tailback, Ronnie Barber was an all-American and had his picture on the cover of Sports Illustrated. I thought Ronnie could get a scholarship to any school he wanted. I was considering a U.S.C. scholarship and had already talked to a professional team.

We were playing against our rival, Banning High, who was last year's City Champion team. It was a big game, and at halftime we were losing 21-10. When halftime was over, we received the kickoff. We marched down the field, and Ronnie almost took it in for a touchdown but got tackled on the eight yard line. It was third down, five to go. I played defensive linebacker, but the coach used me at fullback when we needed a few yards. I was like my hot rod, not that fast at the top end, but I kicked ass off the line.

For the last month I had worked out, sprinting up hills and running in soft sand at the beach. It was time to use that power. We were in the huddle, and Ron called the play. He handed me the ball, I blew though the defensive line, and the score was 21-16. We made the extra point and kicked off. We battled back and forth until there were only five minutes left in the game. Banning punted the ball, we caught it on the five yard line, and got tackled on the ten. The coach called my name, and I was in.

"You want me in there on first down?" I asked the coach.

"We haven't had any success since you made the last TD, so get in there and do your best."

At the tailback position, Ron not only passed the ball but was our best running back. The plan was to keep the defense off guard. I hammered them down the middle, and Ron did his thing. We worked our way to their forty, then we hit a wall. It was third and four, and the coach sent in a play. Ron was going to fake a pass to me, then go for the TD. Shit, I wasn't a receiver, and we never practiced this play. What was the coach thinking? The defensive backs weren't fooled and blitzed. He passed the ball, I caught it. Touchdown. Little did I know that this would be the last play I would ever run, and the end of my football career.

The following Wednesday afternoon, we had a scrimmage with the JVs. My rod wasn't running, and I needed a ride home after practice. A friend and teammate, Randy Brown, offered to give me a ride home in his truck. There were eight of us, three in the cab and five in the back. I jumped in the back with Stanley, a good friend and surfing partner. Randy dropped off a couple of the guys on Twentieth and Averill, then turned left on Twenty-sixth Street. My best friend, Duff, lived at the end of that block, and I lived on Twenty-eighth, three blocks away. I was sitting on the rail behind Randy. We passed Duff's house, and Randy made a sharp right. I lost my grip and balance and flew off the side of the truck bed, landing in the street.

The next thing I remembered was opening my eyes. It

Red Sky Morning

was really bright and sort of blurry. I was lying on my back, and I didn't know where I was. I tried to raise my head to look around, but a sharp pain in my neck stopped me. I heard someone say, "He's awake, he's awake!"

A nurse came into view and asked, "How are you feeling?"

I tried to speak, but my throat was really dry. I tried again. "Sore, and a little dizzy. What happened? Where am I?"

"You fell off a truck and hit your head. You're at San Pedro Hospital, and you've been unconscious for over five hours."

"Wow. I heard some people calling my name. Who's here?"

"There are a lot of people worried about you."

"Can I see them?"

"You feel up to it?"

"Yeah, can you raise me up a little so I can see who's here, and could you get me some water?"

The nurse raised the bed, and I sipped some water out of a flex straw.

There they were, huddled around my bed. My father and my mother, who was crying, and Randy, who was smiling and crying at the same time. My sister and other friends and family were right behind them.

The next morning, Dr. Mathews and another Doctor I didn't recognize paid me a visit.

"Hi, Doc, how's it going?"

"I'm fine. This is Dr. Rosen. He's a neurologist and has been helping me see how you're doing."

"Well, Andy, you're a lucky man. What was explained to me was, you flipped off the side of a truck going twenty-five to thirty miles an hour and landed on the back of your head. You had convulsions, and your friends had to hold you down. In fact, you threw one of your friends over ten feet from you. You're lucky you're alive and didn't end up paralyzed. Surprisingly, your x-rays show no broken bones, cracked skull, or any serious damage to your neck."

"Man, that's great news. When can I start playing football again? I've got to tell the coach."

Dr. Mathews smiled and said, "You're damn lucky you have a thick Slav skull, and that you were in excellent shape, or we might not be talking to each other. I want to talk to you about playing football."

"How long do I have to wait?"

"Dr. Rosen and I feel you shouldn't play."

"You mean for the whole season?"

"No, we mean never again. Andy, if you broke a leg, injured your hand, or something like that, I wouldn't say a thing, but you had a serious concussion, and you're always banging heads at your positions at fullback and linebacker. There is no guarantee that you wouldn't seriously damage yourself. The final decision is yours, but I hope you take our recommendation seriously."

Dr. Mathews had been my doctor most of my life, and I trusted him. So that was it. No football, no scholarships, and no future in pro ball. Fuck, what a bummer.

Chapter 23

A bunch of us were watching the 1964 Rose Bowl game, where Illinois just beat Washington 17-7. I was with my new girlfriend, Mary Cutri. She went to South High and I met her at a friend's party about a month ago. I was graduating in the winter class and I was taking Mary to my prom.

With no scholarship in hand and finishing high school, I decided to enroll at Harbor Jr. College. Mary was still in high school and we eventually drifted apart.

I had classes two days a week and needed a part time job. Some of my family had left commercial fishing and became Longshoremen. Through them, I was able to get a casual card allowing me to work outside the union as a stevedore checker. It was great, went to school, worked when I could, and surfed and partied as much as possible. I finally decided to sell my hot rod. I saved a few bucks, sold the Ford for six hundred dollars, and bought a customized 1956 Karmann Ghia.

This was a time of revolution where young people were breaking out of the molds of their parents.

The Beatles were featured on the Ed Sullivan Show and our world was a'changing.

It was sex, drugs, and rock n' roll, and all of us were right in the middle of it. The spring semester ended. I was happy with three C's and one B, and didn't register for summer school. I turned eighteen in July, and rocked out all summer.

* * *

The next twelve months flew by. The Cultural Revolution exploded. The Beatles got trippier, the Rolling Stones and other bands blossomed. The youth were evolving and becoming more vocal. Subcultures like the Hippies, influenced fashion and values, the entertainment industry, and art.

Then, during President Johnson's administration, we went to war with Vietnam and the youth revolted. The draft increased and people fled to Canada to avoid it. The ones going to college made sure to maintain good grades and to have enough credits to remain exempt from the draft. I hoped to remain in that category until this crazy war ended.

* * *

It was Saturday October 9. Duff and I were sitting on our boards, waiting for the next set to roll in. A hurricane that swept through Baja had pushed up a big south swell, and we decided to surf the point at Cabrillo Beach. It was a good decision; the waves were eight feet, with perfect form. "Can you believe it, there's only four of us out here," Duff said.

"And you wanted to go to Huntington Beach. You know how crowded it would be, and the waves were probably closed out."

Over the next couple of hours the waves got even bigger, and the rides longer. After four hours I was burned out. Duff was paddling back out and came up next to me

"Phew, I'm tired."

"Me too. Let's go in, get something to eat, and catch some rays."

The next set was rolling in. The second wave was huge. I paddled over the first wave, spun my board around, and a few strokes later I was on my last ride of the day.

Duff took the following wave and was right behind me. We dropped off our boards by the lifeguard tower and headed for the grill. We both ordered double cheeseburgers, fries, and Cokes.

As soon as we got our orders, we walked back to the lifeguard tower, where our friends hung out. Many of us had been junior lifeguards and had made friends with the full-timers, who were two to three years older. Some had already finished college, were teaching school, and lifeguarding during the summer. Others were still in high school or going to college. Some of the older guys were longshoremen or fisherman Most of them were single, but a few were married, and even had kids.

We were shooting the shit, about commercial fishing in Mexico, when John Burich asked me how that summer went, fishing with my dad on the East Coast. They all wanted to know the whole story, especially the sex part. When the story got to Boston, I didn't talk about my relationship with Nicole, which was still close to my heart and nobody's business.

By the time I was telling them about the flight back to L.A., and getting my cock caught in my zipper, the whole group was cracking up, then the subject changed to what we were going to do that night.

The weekend flew by, and it was already Tuesday. I just finished dinner, when the phone rang.
My mother answered the phone.
"Andy, it's for you."
I picked up the phone. "Hello."
"Hey, Andy, this is Lou Pappas"
Lou was one of my friends and a lifeguard a Cabrillo Beach. He explained that a mutual friend, Ronnie Misetich's wife, was expecting a child any time now and had asked him to take his place on his dad's fishing boat this weekend. Lou had accepted but subsequently had a death in his family. He couldn't make it and knew I had experience fishing on a purse seiner. He asked if I was interested in taking his place.
"You could make $300-600 in two days if they caught any fish."
"What kind of fish were they catching?"
"Mostly mackerel. Ronnie said that last week they caught forty tons, and he made $700."
"Is the boat going out of San Pedro?"
"No, it's moored up in Port Hueneme."
"How would I get there? Would I have to drive?"
"No, Ronnie's dad, Anton, has a big truck, and the whole crew lives in San Pedro, so they carpool up there. Frank Karmelich is working on the boat, so you'll know at least one person."
I thought, nothing keeping me here next weekend. Frank's a lot of fun, so what the hell, I accepted.
After I hung up the phone, I went to the den to talk to my father. "Hey, Dad, I was asked to take Ronnie Misetich's place fishing on his dad's boat."
"For how long?"
"Thursday to Sunday. You know his dad, don't you?"
"Sure, Anton and I grew up together. He owns the

Diana. Where are they fishing?"

"Out of Port Hueneme. Anton would be driving up there Thursday afternoon, and the whole crew is going up in his truck. What's the *Diana* like?"

"It's a lot smaller than the *Western Ace*. I think it's around eighty-five feet long. Remember my boat, the *Long Island?* It's like that. It's got a single screw and holds around 150 tons of fish. Anyway, you have plenty of experience, and maybe you can make a few bucks. Just be careful."

I decided to call Anton, and let him know I was going.

"Hi, Mr. Misetich. This is Andy Rafkin."

"Yeah, my son called and told me you're taking his place this trip. I know you've got plenty of experience, so I'm glad you're going. By the way, how's your dad?"

"He's fine. He's been home for a couple of weeks. I think he's meeting the *Western Ace* in Panama next week."

"Say hello to him for me. I'll pick you up around one o'clock Thursday. What's your address?"

I gave him my address, and he told me to bring my own boots, and some warm clothes, because it could get pretty cold this time of the year.

Chapter 24

I attended classes Thursday morning and was ready to go by noon. Anton pulled up to my house around one-fifteen and introduced the crew, "This is Bob Lucin, his brother-in-law Nick Dimeglio, and his cousin Ike Ventimiglia, and you know Frank. You'll be riding in the back with Frank and Nick."

"How long will it take to get there?"

"It's about a two and a half hour drive, so keep your jacket handy. It'll get chilly on the way up."

I threw my gear into the back of the truck and jumped in. We sat with our backs against the cab. I was on the driver's side, Frank on the passenger's side, and Nick in the middle. Nick was a full time-crew member, and Frank and I had a lot of questions about fishing this weekend. He was happy to answer them all.

"Hey, Nick, what are we fishing for?" asked Frank.

"We'll be fishing for mackerel, and most of the fish has been caught at night. The fishing has been pretty good, with most boats averaging twenty to sixty tons a day."

I asked, "Where do you unload the fish?"

"Well, if we catch some, we'll head back to Port Hueneme and unload the following morning at the Pan Pacific Cannery.

How much does mackerel go for per ton?"

"The cannery is paying around forty dollars a ton, so after the boat takes its share and covers expenses, our share could range from $100 to $300 a day. Even more, if we get lucky."

"Sounds good to me."

We were traveling up Highway 1, passing through Santa Monica as our conversation faded. This was familiar turf to me, because my buddies and I would drive up here to surf at Malibu. Farther up the coast were Rincon Point, Carpinteria Beach, and more.

My right arm was resting on top of the rail when I suddenly remembered that the last time I was in the back of a truck I had been sitting where my arm was, and as Randy turned right, I went flying off. That thought ran shivers up my spine. I was lucky to be alive. No more football, but better than being dead or crippled for life.

I was trying to shake that thought out of my head when Anton pulled into a gas station. It was around 2:30 and we were ready for a pit stop. The attendant walked up, and Anton told him to fill it up and check the oil. I felt thirsty, so I walked over to the vending machine, put in a quarter, and pulled out a Coke. I offered to buy, and Anton and Frank were the only takers.

Back on the highway, I decided to lie back, enjoy the scenery, and check out the surf. I wondered what the *Diana* was like. I asked Nick.

"You're familiar with the boats your father built. The *Long Island* and the *Sea Scout* are similar to the *Diana*. She was built in the forties to fish for sardines. You know, during the forties and fifties the sardine fishery was huge. That was a great time." Nick seemed to drift off in thought then said,

Red Sky Morning

"Anyway, the *Diana* is close to ninety feet long, and is powered by a 671 Detroit diesel engine. She holds about 140 tons of fish and rides better when she has thirty or forty tons of fish in the hold. She's a little top heavy, so she pitches and rocks a bit when she's empty."

"How long have you worked on the *Diana*?"

"Bob and I started working for Anton almost two years ago, and my cousin, Ike joined us about a year ago."

About an hour after we left the gas station, we pulled up to the cannery dock. The *Diana* was tied up there with five or six other purse seiners. We grabbed our gear and boarded the *Diana*. When I got to the bunk room it became apparent that the accommodations weren't near as nice as on the *Ace*. It really didn't matter, because I was only going to be there for two nights.

As the crew dumped off their gear, they headed for the galley, so I did the same. Bob was the cook and was already working at the counter.

"Hey Bob what's for dinner?" Ike asked.

"I'm gonna roast a couple of chickens, some potatoes, and onions. This morning, I picked up a few loaves of fresh French bread, so I plan to make a nice salad to go with it."

"I'm glad you're starting early, because you know Anton; we'll be the first boat out fishing and the first to make a set."

I stepped out on the deck and lit a cigarette. Nick was right behind me, so I asked him if he wanted a smoke. "Thank you, but you smoke those filtered ones. I like Camels."

"What time are we leaving?"

"Most of the boats will go out around six. But like Ike said, we'll be first to pull out, so be prepared to leave about an hour from now."

"Where are we headed?"

"About an hour and a half run up the coast."

"Frank said that some of the boats were fishing at the Channel Islands."

"That's right, but the fish have moved around seven to ten miles off the coast, and Anton said that's where we were headed. You mind helping me with these cables?"

"Sure, what can I do?"

Nick was the skiff man, and he wanted to position the skiff toward the stern to get it ready for fishing. Nick turned on the winch, and we moved the boom into position. I attached the cable to the bow of the skiff, and Nick wrapped the cable around the winch. As Nick put pressure on the cable, the winch started to pull, and slowly the bow of the skiff lifted up. When the skiff was at a thirty degree angle, it started to slide toward the stern. When Nick felt the skiff was in the right position he asked me to secure the permanent cable to the pelican hook.

"Well that's one less thing I have to do later. Thanks."

Nick was right on, because at five sharp, I heard the old diesel engine fire up. Smoke billowed out of the stack, and after a couple of minutes, the rough sound of the engine became smoother. I thought if my car sounded like that, I'd plan to get rid of it.

The *Diana* had an open bridge, where you could see Anton standing at the wheel. He turned and yelled, "It's time to go. Andy, stand by on the bow line." Ike already had the stern line free. Anton put it in reverse and used the bow line to swing out into the bay. As the stern moved out, he pushed it forward, and the bow closed to the dock.

Anton yelled, "Let'er go."

I unhooked the rope from the cleat on the dock and jumped onto the boat. Anton put it in reverse, and we slowly backed out into the harbor. As soon as we were clear, he pushed the throttle forward and steered out through the jetty.

The weather was beautiful, clear, and calm as slick

Red Sky Morning

grease. The sunset was awesome. *This trip is going to be all right.* I went down to the bunkroom to get my gear ready. I had my rain slicks and hip boots. I noticed where the crew put their gear on deck, so I pulled on my boots and put my rain gear with theirs.

I saw Nick climb out of the skiff and jump off the pile of net. He was the head crewman, and I wanted to know what was expected of me.

"Hey, Nick, everything OK?"

"Yeah, just making my final rounds. You know how fast things start to go when you hear 'Mola Mola'. It's dangerous enough without any unexpected problems. When that skiff drops off the stern, with one side of the net attached, any cable or rope in the wrong place could get tangled, pulling somebody overboard. If that happened, he'd probably get killed."

"When I worked on the *Western Ace,* one of my jobs was to check the ropes and cabling for that same reason."

Bob stuck his head out the galley door and yelled, "Dinner's ready." Nick relieved Anton, who joined us for dinner. Anton rushed through his meal and went back to the bridge.

Nick joined us and said, "Better hurry, the skipper seems anxious. I wouldn't be surprised if we make our first set within an hour."

Nick took a sip of *vino*, and turned to Bob, "I was talking to Andy about the old days when we fished for sardines.

"That was a great time. There were millions of tons caught a year. We caught sardines all up and down the coast. You know, it was the biggest industry on the West Coast."

Bob smiled. "Remember when we fished off of San Francisco, and when we went into port, they treated the fishermen like kings. The restaurants on the pier couldn't do enough for us. Sometimes they would close the doors to the public, and we would have a big party. Wine, women, and song.

"Remember when we came into Monterey with a deckload of sardines. We had so much fish piled up, I thought we were going to sink," said Nick.

"I remember standing on the dock with my mom, waiting for my dad's boat to come in. The deck was full of sardines up to the top of the rail. Most of the hull was under water, and I always wondered how it stayed afloat."

"Well, the captains knew what their boats could handle," was Nick's response. "There were times when one boat would make a set, and there was so much fish in the net that it could have swamped the boat. Sometimes, two or three boats could load up on the sardines in that one net. There were floating processing plants where we could unload the fish. That way, we could stay out longer and catch more. If we were close to ports like San Francisco, Monterey, and of course our home port, San Pedro, we would unload there. When in port, we would refuel, get groceries, and in San Pedro we would spend time with our families."

I was enjoying their stories and watching them get excited about the past. These guys, these fishermen, had led a tough life and yet, loved every minute of it. I could see it in their eyes, a look I've seen before.

Nick was right again, because around thirty minutes had gone by, then Anton was yelling for us to get ready.

"Mola Mola!" Frank hit the pelican hook, and the skiff went off the stern, dragging one side of the net. I was surprised how fast we completed the circle, closed the gap, and had the net running through the power block. Frank, Ike, and I started stacking the net. When I was on the *Ace* it took almost an hour to restack the net. We finished in about half that time, but it dawned on me that we weren't going any faster. It was just a smaller boat and a shorter net. The twine used to make this net was a lot thinner, and the mesh was much smaller because the fish we were catching were no longer than a foot. Tuna on the other hand, can very from five to 250 pounds, so the mesh is much bigger and so is the diameter of the twine.

When we had most of the net piled, it became obvious that we didn't have any fish in it. Oh well, it was a dry run, but I now felt comfortable and ready for the next set. We didn't have wait to long before I heard, "Mola Mola."

I used to like that command because it usually meant more fish and more money, but after being skunked three times in a row, I was starting to hate it.

Mola Mola number four, we actually caught some fish, only two or three tons, but it was a start. Number five came and went with no fish, and number six followed suit.

I said to Nick, "This guy's Mola Mola crazy."

Nick laughed. "I told you so."

It was past midnight, and I was exhausted. The hell with the extra money, I just wanted to go to sleep. Well, that wasn't going to happen, because I heard the old diesel speed up, so I knew number seven was coming up. Lucky number seven; God, I hope so.

Number seven came through. More than two-thirds of the net was in and we started to see fish. We bunched up the net and started to brail the mackerel aboard. I began to feel a lot better. Now I was making money.

Number seven brought in around twenty tons, and then came number eight, and we really caught some fish.

It was 4:00 A.M., and we were still brailing fish. I asked Ike how many tons in this set.

"Around thirty-five, maybe forty. You getting tired?"

"Totally. When we finish this, will we continue fishing?"

"Lucky for you and for all of us, after this we will be headed to port. On the way in, try to get some rest, because we'll be going directly to the cannery to unload."

"When do we get to sleep?"

"When there's nothing to do."

"Well, maybe after we finish unloading."

"Don't count on it. I overheard Anton talking to the cannery foreman. He said that we might go straight back to the fishing area and see if we might find some fish during the day, and if Anton mentioned it, we'll be heading back out as soon as we can."

"God, what a slave driver. Guess we'll get some rest on the way out."

"Andy, I hope so, because I'm beat, and so is everybody else."

We cleaned up the deck and secured the gear. All I wanted to do was hit the bunk. I washed my hands and face, kicked off my boots, and jumped in. I tossed and turned for almost an hour, but I couldn't get to sleep. I wasn't used to working all night, and my inner clock was telling me it was almost time to get up, so that's what I did. It was five-thirty in the morning, and I felt like shit. I went into the galley, poured myself a cup of coffee, and sat down. I grabbed a deck of cards and played solitaire.

After a couple of cups of coffee and losing three games, I decide to go out on deck and have a cigarette. It was chilly outside, so I went back to my bunk and pulled on a sweatshirt, then went up to the bow. The sun was starting to rise, and I could see lights on shore, probably Port Hueneme.

"Hey, Andy, how's it going?"

"Oh, hi, Frank. Just having a smoke and watching the sun rise. I couldn't sleep, so here I am."

"I had the same problem. I guess I'm not used to working all night. Talk about some sunrise."

The whole eastern sky was painted in red and orange, and Frank and I stood silent, watching the beginning of a new day.

"Bob was getting up when I left the bunkroom; he said he

was going to whip up some breakfast. I don't know about you, but I'm starved."

"I'm with you. Let's get something to eat."

Bob was frying some ham and asked us if we wanted some eggs. "Sunny side up for me." Frank ordered over easy.

"You'll have to settle for scrambled. I'm not a short-order cook, you know."

Ike and Nick walked in and sat down. They knew the drill and ate what was given to them. I was just about finished with breakfast when the old Detroit diesel slowed down. That meant we were getting close to our destination.

When we got out on deck, the cannery was coming up on the starboard side. One other boat was unloading fish, and Anton pulled in behind her, in front of the unloading equipment on the dock. We secured the lines and uncovered the main hatch of the fish hold. The opening was around ten feet square, covered with two-by-twelve inch planks. One by one, we removed them, and stacked them on the portside deck.

Unloading mackerel was totally different from unloading tuna. The cannery workmen lowered a flexible pipe, around a foot in diameter, into the fish hold, then a large hose. The big pipe was attached to a huge vacuum machine. The water came on, and Ike kept the stream in front of the pipe's opening. When the vacuum was turned on, it would suck up the mackerel and water. The fish passed through the vacuum onto a conveyor, and off to processing. The process was clean, efficient, and fast. It wasn't long before the equipment was pulled back on the dock, and as Nick predicted, we were pulling away.

Chapter 25

The *Diana* moved slowly ahead as Anton maneuvered her through the channel. On one side of the channel, commercial fishing boats were tied up to the dock, and the other side, yachts were tied up to their moorings at Port Hueneme Yacht Club. It was still early in the morning, and there wasn't any activity in the harbor.

I lit a cigarette and walked up to the bow. The *Diana* was entering the bay and headed for the opening of the breakwater. I could hear the old diesel engine starting to pick up speed. I saw Anton at the wheel, the smoke billowing out of the stack behind him.

As we left the protection of the jetties, the *Diana* started to roll over two to three-foot swells. There was a slight offshore breeze, and it was chilly. The sun was shining, and it was perfectly clear, except for the wispy clouds in the sky that produced that reddish-orange glow which made the spectacular sunrise Frank and I witnessed.

As soon as I leaned on the railing and started to relax, I felt every aching muscle in my body. I felt little dizzy from lack of sleep. I flicked my cigarette into the water and headed for the bunkroom.

Everybody was already asleep and snoring away. I climbed into my bunk and thought, I'll never get to sleep with all this snoring. I started listening to the different sounds that the guys made. It sounded like a strange type of music. Bob at alto and loud, Frank at tenor, Ike sort of whistling, and Nick grunting, like sort of keeping a beat. I wished I had a tape recorder. It couldn't have been more than a few seconds before I conked out.

Someone was shaking me. I must have been dreaming.

"Andy wake up." No, I wasn't dreaming. That's Nick's voice.

"What's going on?"

"Anton spotted a school of mackerel. Time to go to work."

"Shit, what time is it?"

"9:00 A.M."

"Only an hour of sleep. No wonder I feel like crap."

Ten minutes later; "Mola Mola," and we were off and running. Nick was right, when he said Anton would set on one fish. When we were almost finished stacking the net, you could see there was only a hundred pounds of fish in it, so we dumped them out and got ready for the next set.

I thought I was tired before, but after three more sets and no fish, I was not only totally burned out, but really disappointed. It was apparent that the fish were surfacing only at night, and that we were wasting our time.

Anton climbed down from the bridge and said, "This is bullshit. I think we'll run up to the oil rigs, anchor on the lee side of one of the islands, and get some rest. We'll go out later. Maybe we'll be luckier tonight."

There was a big sigh from the crew, because it was only noon, and the man-made islands were located on the east side of the Santa Barbara coast, so we had only a few miles to go. During the next hour we straightened out the rigging and had lunch. I was helping Bob clean up the kitchen when the old diesel engine started to slow down.

Anton yelled, "Get ready to drop the anchor."

Frank and Nick went to the bow and got ready.

"Let 'er go!" yelled Anton.

Nick released the winch, and the anchor dropped into the water, pulling the chain behind it. Anton put the *Diana* in reverse, and Nick let out enough chain, so the anchor would dig into the bottom. Anton made sure that the anchor was secured, shifted out of reverse, and shut down the engine.

It was time to get some rest. The crew trooped off to the bunkroom, and I decided to go up on the bridge and catch some rays while I slept. I took off my shirt, rolled it up to use as a pillow, and sprawled out on the deck. I could hear the seagulls squawking and the seals barking in the distance. The gentle rolling of the boat and the familiar sounds of the sea got me thinking of the summer's adventure on the *Ace*.

Flying through a hurricane, a night with Rosa, surfing through a jetty in a twenty-four-foot boat, plowing through a rogue wave, on the beach with Lauren, almost run over by a cruise ship, fishing, friends, and then Nicole. I could see her smiling at me as I faded into a deep sleep.

I woke up with a start. I was freezing. There was a cold offshore wind blowing. I had surfed this area a few times, and an offshore wind was normal and cold. There were some awesome surfing spots close to where we had anchored. One place nearby was Rincon Point. Last winter, Duff and I spent two days there, surfing perfect six to eight-foot waves. The strong offshore wind held up the face of the waves, giving you a long tubular ride. They were some of the best waves I had ever ridden. A chill went up my back, and it wasn't about surfing the waves. It was because

I was shivering. Time to go down to the bunkroom.

I thought the snoring was loud this morning, but the band was roaring. I jumped into my bunk and warmed up under my blanket. The music didn't bother me, and a couple minutes later I'm sure I joined in. I woke up to the crew talking and getting dressed.

"What's up?" I asked.

Nick answered, "Its four o'clock, time to go fishing."

I climbed out of my bunk and started to get dressed. Ike said, "Better put on some warm clothes, it's going to be a cold night." I pulled on jeans, and a sweatshirt, then my hip boots, which I folded down to my knees.

The offshore breeze that woke me earlier was much stronger and felt colder. The captain said, "It's four o'clock. Nick it's time to pull up the anchor and go fishing."

"Hey, Andy, give me a hand with the anchor."

Nick got the winch going and started to pull up the anchor. I made sure that the chain was going down in the storage hold neatly. The wind felt stronger, and when the anchor was off the bottom we started drifting towards the island, catching Anton off guard. He was cussing in Croatian while he attempted to start the engine. Just when I thought we were going to drift onto the rocks, the old diesel turned over, belched a couple of times, and slowly moved us away from disaster.

I climbed up to the bridge and walked over to Anton. "Andy, how's it going?"

"Doing good. What do you think about this weather?"

"The weather's been good the last few days, and I listened to the marine forecast earlier. It called for moderate weather tonight and tomorrow."

When we passed the last oil rig and were about a mile out, it started to get rough. We took a couple of swells over the bow, and I looked at Anton.

"It's a little choppy, nothing to worry about." I figured if the captain isn't worried about the weather, then neither should I.

We talked a few minutes about our families, and how excited Anton was about becoming a grandfather. He asked me if I intended to become a fisherman. Of course my answer was no, that I planned to graduate from college and get a good job. He said that was a good idea, because the fishing industry was getting worse, and a fisherman's life was rough and dangerous.

The weather looked to be taking a turn for the worse, but Anton didn't appear concerned. I decided to go to the galley, so I asked the skipper if he wanted anything. He said he was fine, so I left the bridge.

Ike and Frank were sitting at the table, and Bob was trying to secure everything in the kitchen. "Where's Nick?" I asked.

"In the engine room," answered Frank.

Ike said, "You were up talking to Anton. Is he planning to try to fish in this shit?"

"I think so. What do you think?"

"I just looked at the barometer, and it's dropping, which means the weather could get worse."

Bob jumped in, "I know this area. We're still protected by the coastal mountains, but when we get out a few more miles, it will get worse. Between the mainland and the Channel Islands, the water is shallow, maybe fourteen to thirty fathoms. This ocean can get nasty real fast."

The *Diana* shuddered, then leaned so far to port that Frank almost fell off the bench, and stuff was sliding off the table. Nick was out of the engine room and in the galley in one second.

"What the hell's going on?"

The *Diana* was bouncing back and forth between the

waves. This time, another wave knocked us so far over that Frank slipped and fell to the deck, while dishes and pans were rolling all over the place.

Frank yelled, "This damn boat is top heavy, and we're running empty. This isn't good. I'm going up to talk to Anton."

"I'm not staying down here. I want to see what's going on," I shouted.

That's all it took, and we all made for the bridge.

I couldn't believe how much stronger the wind was since I left the bridge earlier. I figured it was blowing around forty to fifty miles per hour. The swells were six to ten feet high, they were steep, close together, and already cresting and breaking.

It all happened so fast it caught, even this experienced skipper by surprise. We must have passed that three-mile mark that Bob was talking about, because the wind velocity had to have increased by twenty or thirty percent, and the waves were increasingly bigger.

It was really getting scary. Water was coming over the bow—not spray but solid green water. Nick was right; the Diana was high in the water and top heavy. We were being pitched back and forth so fast it was hard to keep my balance. The waves grew to fifteen feet plus, cresting and breaking.

Nick yelled to Anton, "What do you want to do?"

"It's getting worse, we need to turn around, get the swell on our ass end, and head for Hueneme"

"Anton, if one of these fucking waves catches us broadside, it could capsize us."

"Nothing to be worried about; she's a good boat."

I thought, *CAPSIZE! What the hell are they saying?* I was really scared, and by looking at the rest of the crew's faces, they felt the same.

Red Sky Morning

The skipper tried over and over again to turn around. As we went over one breaking swell, he would start the turn, but the trough between waves was so narrow that if he continued turning, the next wave would catch us broadside. Anton had to spin the wheel back in attempt to be directly facing the next wave. I was impressed at how well Anton handled the *Diana*. Timing was everything, and when we were a little off, we would pay for it. The *Diana* would heel so far over, all we could do was hang on and pray.

The wind was blowing harder, and the waves were getting bigger, at least twenty feet or more. Anton was having a hard time, and I could see the fear in his eyes. The *Diana* rose over the next swell and started to turn, when one huge breaking wave came at us.

"Oh my God, we're going over!" Nick screamed.

I braced myself and hung on as the wave engulfed the *Diana*, and we started to slide up its face. The crest hit the starboard bow, and broke over the bridge. Shit was breaking and flying all over the place. The *Diana* was on her side, and I thought, man, it's all over, but somehow she rode herself upright, and kept going.

At that point, Anton wasn't trying to turn around. He was just trying to survive. A few terrifying seconds went by, and another huge breaking wave came straight at us. We went up its face and Anton pushed the throttle forward. The wave covered the bridge; I lost my footing, and hung on for life. As we cleared that wave, I could see the next wave roaring at us. What I saw scared the shit out of me, because the following wave was much bigger.

We braced ourselves as the next wave slammed into us. The *Diana* took it straight on and did her job, but the next wave was on her so fast that it knocked us over on our portside. She tried to ride herself up again, but there wasn't enough time.

We were almost lying broadside, in the trough, facing a huge and ugly wave. The *Diana* was starting to come about as we started up the face. Anton had one hand on the wheel and the other pushing the throttle, hoping there was more power in that old engine.

We all realized she wasn't going up the face, but falling more to the portside. The crest of the wave broke over us, and we were so far over I could see the ocean surface bellow. Oh God help us, We Were Capsizing!

I was hanging onto the port railing when we went over. I lost my grip and was catapulted overboard. I literally flew through the air and I hit the water hard. I was a good swimmer, but for some reason I couldn't stay upright. I remembered I had on hip boots and realized that they had flipped up onto my thighs and were full of air. When a wave went by, I almost flipped upside down.

I tried to try to kick my boots off, then instead of being full of air, they filled up with water and pulled me down. I took a deep breath, held it, and while I was underwater, tried to kick my left boot off. It seemed to take forever, but I finally got it off.

I must have been ten feet below the surface and almost out of oxygen. I kicked and pulled with my arms as hard as I could, finally breaking the surface and gasping for air. I knew I had to get the other boot off so I concentrated on my task, took a couple of deep breaths, and went after it.

They say one foot is bigger than the other. Well, I had a hell of a time getting off that boot, but after the third time underwater and back for air, it was off, and I was dog-paddling.

All I could think of was self-preservation and looked up to get my bearings. The giant waves, along with the current and the wind, had pushed me farther from the *Diana;* I figured I was over two hundred feet away. I thought it was all over, then I spotted something floating nearby. It was the freezer from the bridge, and its lid was wide open. I swam as hard as I could, got to it, and slammed the lid shut. I climbed on top and hung on.

I felt a strange but familiar feeling of being really alone. I remembered I felt that way when I was alone on the speedboat in those giant swells off the East Coast. I was scared and started to cry, figuring it wouldn't be long before my life was over.

Shit this isn't fair, I'm only nineteen, and this isn't even my real job.

I was three to four hundred feet from the *Diana* and the first time I had a chance to take a good look at her. She wasn't sinking but on her side, the mast lying on the surface. I could see the rudder, and I couldn't believe it, but the prop was still turning.

I saw someone walking on the side of the boat. Another crewman—I think it was Nick—joined him. He had a hammer or an axe in his hand and they both were headed toward the stern.

About a hundred feet away, I could see the net and corks floating on the surface. There was someone floating on top of the corks that he had bunched up below him.

The skiff! Where in the hell was the skiff? If it was close, I could swim to it. Easy enough to pull myself onto it. I looked in every direction, but no skiff.

I saw Nick start chopping a cable with the axe and realized what he was doing. The skiff must have sunk when the *Diana* went over, and he was trying to cut the cable that was attached to it. The *Diana* wasn't sinking, at least not yet, so maybe they thought the skiff was holding them down.

Nick must have chopped through the cable, because the mast started to rise out of the water. It started to lift and lift, then to my amazement, the *Diana* rode herself upright.

I knew I had just witnessed a miracle!

The only thing I could think of now was to swim back to the *Diana*, which was now even farther away. I swam almost everyday, and I felt I could make the distance, but swimming through twenty-foot breaking waves was almost too much.

Slow down, pace yourself.

As I neared the net, I recognized Ike, who had gathered up some corks under him to stay afloat. I thought about trying to help him, but I decided it would be better to save my own skin first.

The *Diana* was now 150 feet away. As I got closer, I could see Anton, Frank, and Nick. They were yelling and waving their arms. I stopped swimming and tried to hear them. I heard, "Bob" then, "help Bob." I waved, and they pointed to my right. I turned and saw Bob hanging on the rope with the corks on it, secured to the *Diana*, and attached to the net floating behind me.

I swam toward Bob, who was now about fifty feet away. I was starting to get tired and realized the cold water was draining my strength. The rope and corks were closer to me than Bob, so I decided to go there first, then I'd worry about Bob. It seemed to take forever to reach the rope, but when my hand touched it, I knew my chances of survival had increased. I got a boost of energy, and hand over hand, I worked myself towards the *Diana*.

Bob was between me and the boat. It was difficult to hold on. Half the time I was underwater as a wave broke over me, then I was halfway out of the water when the trough passed by. The corks helped me stay afloat, and I was now in arm's reach of Bob. The look on his face scared the hell out of me. His eyes and mouth were wide open, and he looked like he was trying to scream. I yelled at him, but he wouldn't or couldn't answer me. I thought he must be in shock. He had both hands gripped on the rope, and I had to free his grip in order to pull him to the *Diana*. I couldn't believe what a tight grip he had. I literally had to peel each finger off the rope.

Now that he was free, I wondered what the hell I was going to do with him. He was unconscious and about my size, and totally dead weight. I decided to lock my legs around his chest and under his arms, so my hands were free to work hand over hand toward the *Diana*.

When we went through a wave, I held my breath and hung on. No matter how hard I gripped the rope, the waves slid it through my hands. The closer I got to the *Diana*, the steeper the angle of the rope became, because the rope was six feet above the waterline, coming over the rail.

The waves were knocking Bob and me all over the place. As we got closer, there were times when we were underwater, and as the trough passed under us, Bob and I were dangling, suspended in midair.

I had no idea where my strength was coming from, but somehow I was doing it. Nick was yelling, "We're going to put a ladder over the side. Hang on!"

My back was facing the hull, and I couldn't figure how to get Bob loose and to the ladder. We were so close to the side of the hull that if I didn't time it just right, the bottom of the boat would crush us.

Nick climbed over the side, hanging onto the ladder, and Frank and Anton hung over the rail. Nick yelled, "Hand him over to me."

What the hell was he thinking? How could I do that?

The rope was about six feet from the ladder, and there was no way I could hand Bob over. I had to do something soon, because I couldn't hang on much longer.

"Move the ladder closer!" I yelled.

Nick yelled back, "We can't. There's nothing to secure it to."

I decided that the only way this would work would be, when we went underwater I would release my legs, grab his right arm with my right hand, and hang on the rope with my left. I planned to use the momentum of the next wave passing under the hull to help pull Bob up.

I yelled my plan to Nick and told him to get as close as he could to the rope and get ready. The timing had to be right on, and I yelled, "NOW!" As I went underwater, I reached down, grabbed Bob's wrist, and released my legs. We rushed upward. I have no idea how I managed to reach out far enough for them to grab Bob, but they did. I let go of him and wrapped my arms and legs around the rope and slid down a few feet.

I heard someone screaming, "Bob! Oh God, no, Bob!"

I looked back at Nick, and Bob wasn't there. Somehow they had lost their grip or something. Jesus, what the hell happened? I looked below me. Bob was floating on his back, looking right at me, with the same look he had when I first got to him. I realized he was dead, and that he was probably already dead when I first pried his fingers off the rope. That was really a death grip. Oh God, I wanted to scream, but nothing came out. I was scared out of my wits.

I had to pull myself together and try to save my own life. My hands hurt like hell. They were all cut up and bleeding. A breaking wave ripped me away from my lifeline. I surfaced and sucked in some air when the next wave hit me. I was tumbling around and hit a rope. My lifeline! While I was submerged, I grabbed the rope and hung on. When I broke the surface, I was twenty feet from the hull. I knew there was no way I could make it up the rope to the railing, so the only way was to let go of the rope and swim to the ladder. I left the only security I had— the rope.

Red Sky Morning

The *Diana* was thrashing all over the place. I kept away from the stern so I wouldn't get crushed under the hull. All I could see was the ladder, and I swam directly to it. The ladder wasn't long enough to get my feet on a step, but I hung on with my hands. Nick was yelling for me to climb up, so I started pulling myself up, step by step.

I felt whatever strength I had left was diminishing rapidly. I looked up at Nick, who was hanging over the rail, and Frank and Anton were hanging on to Nick. He was screaming, "Climb, Goddamn it! Climb, pull. C' mon, Andy, you can make it."

I let out a yell and went for the next step. My right hand caught the step and I brought up my left. I felt Frank's hand, and he screamed, "Grab my hand!"

There was no way. I had no strength left, and my hands were starting to slip.

I screamed, "I'm slipping. Help!"

Nick yelled, "Lower me some more."

My right hand slipped off, and at the same time, Nick grabbed my sweatshirt and slowly pulled me up. I felt my foot hit a step, I got both feet on it, and my hands firmly gripped, then with Nick's assistance, I climbed up. All three guys pulled me over the rail, and laid me on the deck. I tried to get up, but I couldn't move. I could move my head, and I could see, but I couldn't move my arms or legs.

I heard Anton yelling at Nick, "How are we going to get Ike out of the net?"

"I don't know. He looks tangled up, and it's so rough out there, it looks impossible to get to him."

"I've got to try."

"What the hell are you doing? Jesus Christ, Anton, don't. You're going to kill yourself."

I was able to turn my head and looked up just in time to see Anton, a knife in his teeth, dive over the side, apparently to try to save Ike.

I was still lying on the deck. I was alert, but I still couldn't move any part of my body. I could feel tears rolling out of my eyes, and I didn't know what was wrong with me, except that I was in shock or something.

Nick yelled, "Shit, I knew Anton shouldn't have gone overboard. He's tangled up in the net."

"Where is he? I can't see him?" Frank yelled. Oh, there he is. Look's like he's trying to cut himself loose."

"Thank God he took that knife with him, or he would have been a goner. Let's get to the ladder and pull him out."

Frank and Nick pulled Anton over the rail. He lay on the deck next to me, and asked, "How you doing?"

I had a hard time saying anything. I was trying to talk, but nothing was coming out. I eventually said, "I think I'm OK, but I can't seem to move my arms or legs."

"Don't worry, you'll be all right. Just lay there and rest."

Anton got up and was talking to Nick. In the background, I could hear Frank yelling, "Mayday, Mayday!" I couldn't believe it, but the radio was still working.

I lay on the deck listening to the fury of the freak storm, the wind whistling through the rigging, the deck awash. Someone grabbed my shoulder, and I recognized Frank's voice.

"Andy, we need your help"

He pulled me up shook me, and repeated himself. I can't explain it, but I jumped up to my feet, ready to go. God, just seconds earlier, I couldn't move a muscle. It was a miracle.

Then, another miracle. The engine was still running! Nick came out of the galley door and said, "I can't believe it. I just left the engine room. All the batteries and everything else is on the deck, but the engine is still running. On what, I don't know."

The deck was covered with debris, and the windows were broken. The *Diana* was taking a beating, but somehow stayed upright. I was leaning on the main hatch when I realized that all the wooden planks were still in place, unsecured by anything. I couldn't believe it! When the *Diana* was on her side, those planks should have fallen off, and if they had the water would have filled the fish hold. The *Diana* would have gone to the bottom. I guess it just wasn't our time. At least not yet anyway.

Next problem: How to get Ike out of the net and back on deck.

Anton got back to the helm and put the *Diana* in gear. He tried to maneuver so we were close enough to reach Ike, but the wind was blowing sixty to seventy knots, and the ocean had become an ugly monster, huge breaking waves battering the *Diana*.

"It's getting dark, and we have to get Ike out before the sun goes down," Nick yelled to Anton.

Anton tried to maneuver the boat downwind from where Ike was tangled up in the net so the waves would not push the boat over him. We were all on the bow, and when we finally got close, we could hear him call out, "Mommy, Mommy, help me." He was obviously delirious and in shock. Hypothermia was setting in. Ike was over fifty years old, and was in no way a mommy's boy.

Frank was trying to throw Ike a rope, but it was blowing so hard that the rope flew right back. "We have to get closer, and we need some kind of weight on the end of the rope to be able to get it to Ike," Frank yelled.

Nick yelled, "To get closer, we have to cut the rope attached to the net, so we can maneuver better."

While Nick was cutting the rope, Frank and I looked for

a rope with a weight on it. We found a rope with a hook on one end that was heavy enough.

Nick told the skipper what we had in mind, and he steered the *Diana* down wind from the net that was now drifting loose. This time he was able to get a lot closer. Frank threw the weighted line, and the hook flew right over Ike's head. I yelled, "Good shot." It was hard to see if Ike grabbed the line, because the waves were covering him most of the time. I got to the rail and pulled on the rope. As one wave cleared we could see that Ike had tied the rope to his left arm. It was time to pull Ike out. There were three of us; I was at the rail, then Nick, and Frank at the rear.

We started to pull, but Ike was tangled in the net more than we thought. There were three of us on one side and Ike's arm on the other. When a wave smashed into the bow, the rope burned as it slipped through our grip. I thought we might pull Ike's arm right out of his body. We kept trying, and about the fifth time a wave hit us, Ike popped out of the net. We heard the twine snap as he broke loose. We started pulling him in as fast as we could, when the rope unraveled off his arm. Ike was frantically trying to stay afloat, but in seconds he started going under.

Nick freaked out and started screaming, "Oh God, Ike! Oh God."

I don't know what possessed me to start pulling on the rope, but I did. I suddenly felt something on the other end, and it felt heavy. I started pulling as hard as I could.

"Ike is still here! Help me," I screamed.

Frank jumped behind me, and we started to pull him in. Another miracle! The rope with the hook had somehow looped around Ike's leg. We pulled him up feet first. He was unconscious, and his lips were blue. My Junior Lifeguard experience automatically kicked in, and I started giving him mouth-to-mouth resuscitation.

"Andy, it's no use he's gone." Nick thought his cousin was dead, and continued crying.

"No, no way." I yelled. I kept going, pressing on his chest, blowing in fresh air. It felt like a long time had gone by, and I began to think he might be dead. Suddenly he coughed, and threw up a ton of salt water. He slowly began to regain consciousness. Ike was really banged up and complaining about his back.

"We need to get him inside," yelled Nick.

Frank ran to the bunk room and got some blankets. We slid a blanket under him and carefully carried him into the galley. We put him on the galley table and wrapped him in the rest of the blankets.

The sun had gone down, and it was getting dark. I could hear Anton talking to the Coast Guard. He was trying to give them our position, but there was all kinds of static on the radio. Anton was cussing and screaming into the mike. "Shit, I lost them."

Then the static started again, and we heard, "Coast Guard—" then a bunch of static, then "chopper—" then static, then, "boat was—" then a bunch of static, then silence.

Finally, the old diesel belched and died. The lights, the radio, everything went out. With no power, we were at the mercy of the storm. All we could do was hang on, and keep Ike from falling off the table.

"Where are our life jackets?" Frank asked.

"They're topside, Nick said."I'll go get them."

"Be careful," yelled Anton.

A couple of minutes went by, and Nick came through the door. "They're gone! The whole storage box is gone. Probably broke loose when we capsized."

Without warning, the *Diana* twisted and turned violently. It felt like we were in the middle of a whirlpool. She listed so far to port that I was certain we were going over. We all hung on for dear life. *God, we've already experienced a couple of miracles, but we really need your help now.*

A long time passed, then Frank saw the spotlight of a helicopter circling near us. "Mother of God, they found us!"

They were hovering in the distance. We could barely see them, but it looked liked they were pulling something out of the water. We could just make it out, but it was a body.

"It must be Bob's body. Thank God, Nick yelled. We all stared at the scene in shock. None of us could believe they spotted him or found us.

The chopper moved toward us and hovered over the *Diana*. I thought they were going to take us all aboard, but they were there to pick up Ike and get him to the hospital. One of the Coast Guard guys got on the bullhorn and said that a cutter was on its way to help us.

"I'll need your help to get the *Diana* back to port," said Anton, looking at the rest of us.

Shit, this isn't my boat or my job. I was only taking someone's place.

We lifted Ike into the gurney, and they started to pull him up. All I wanted to do was jump and grab the cable, so I could ride up with him and get the hell out of there. But I didn't.

Chapter 26

After the Coast Guard chopper left, we went into the galley for shelter. The wind was still blowing at hurricane force, and the waves were pummeling us. With no fish in the hold, the net and skiff gone, the *Diana* was bobbing around like a cork. There were many times that I thought she was going to flip over. The galley table was secured to the deck, and the four of us huddled together, hanging on.

Nobody said anything, and the three men sitting with me looked totally exhausted and scared. Anton broke down and cried out, "Oh God, why did this happen? Oh Bob, oh Ike, and their families." He continued sort of mumbling something and crying, then Nick broke down while Frank and I just sat there, stunned.

All the windows in the galley were broken, and the wind was whistling through.

"Christ, I'm freezing." I was shivering.

"So am I," said Nick.

All of us were shaking and in some state of shock. Anton got up and went to the bunk room. He came back with a bunch of blankets, and we wrapped ourselves in them.

"I'm still fucking cold," stuttered Frank.

Anton got up again and went back to the bunk room, but this time he brought out a couple of fifths of VO. We drank out of the bottles, taking a swig and passing it on. I was too scared to feel any buzz, but the booze did warm me up and seemed to calm my nerves.

Over an hour passed before we saw the Coast Guard vessel's lights. I never felt so happy and relieved, but still scared out of my wits at the same time. The Coast Guard cutter was about 120 feet long, and as she came alongside the captain stepped out of the bridge and yelled to us through a bullhorn, "Is everyone OK?"

"Yes," yelled Anton.

"We're going to throw you a tow rope. Secure it to your bow, and we'll tow you to Port Hueneme."

One of the sailors threw us a rope, and we pulled in the tow line that was attached to it. We secured it to the bow winch, and they started to tow us back to Port Hueneme. The going was slow, but we were being towed downwind, and with the swell. That made the ride a little better, but we were still not out of danger. By that time, I just didn't give a shit, because we continued to drink the VO, and I now had a good buzz going.

During the next few hours, we got thrown all over the place. There were times when I thought the *Diana* would just break apart, but somehow she held together, and finally we saw the lights of Port Hueneme.

The swells were getting huge, maybe twenty feet plus. One of the sailors on a bullhorn and said they couldn't tow us through the jetty, because the waves were breaking all the way across the opening. He said, if we tried we would either capsize or crash into the breakwater. He said to stand by.

A few minutes later, the bullhorn squawked, "The captain

wants to attempt to surf through the opening. To accomplish this, we need to tie up along side each other. Anton waved to acknowledge their plan.

They threw us the lines and started to maneuver closer. It was so rough that we started slamming into the cutter's hull. We were in an eighty-foot, wooden hull boat, and they were in a one hundred and twenty foot, steel-hulled vessel. After the third time we slammed into their hull, I thought we were going to break apart. It wasn't working, and we were drifting extremely close to shore. In the distance, we could hear the waves breaking on the beach, and both boats were critically close to disaster. We released the lines, secured another tow line, and the Coast Guard cutter pulled us back out to sea.

The captain got on the bullhorn, "This is Captain Redden. I'm sorry, but we can't get in here. The only alternative is to tow you back up the coast to Ventura Harbor, where the entrance is more protected."

"OK, let's go," Yelled Anton.

At that point, we were so close to shore that I felt like jumping overboard and swimming to the beach, but of course I didn't. SHIT! I didn't want to go back out there, and to make things worse, we would be towed another twenty miles facing those horrendous waves.

We were under tow again and headed towards Ventura. I felt so helpless, and I think we all felt the same way. The only thing we could do was hang on and pray that the *Diana* would hold together.

It took over three hours to reach Ventura Harbor. During that time, I thought about my family and how close I came to dying. I worried that my parents might hear about this over the radio or on TV, and not know who was hurt or dead.

Little did I know that they had found out much earlier. My parents went to a friend's house for dinner. Tony Bozanich was also a fisherman and knew Anton. Before my parents arrived, he was watching the news about the *Diana*, and another large ship that was in trouble due to the freak storm. The news reported that the Coast Guard was on site, and that there was a fatality and injuries on the *Diana*. They wouldn't give out any names until relatives were notified.

When my parents arrived at the Bozanich's home for dinner, Elizabeth and Tony told them about the incident. My mother screamed and passed out on the floor. After she came to, they all drove back to my parents' house and waited for a call, hopefully from me.

The weather never let up, and I still felt that we might not make it. I prayed for us. Frank, Nick, and I didn't stop praying until we finally got inside the protection of the breakwater. The craziness was almost over. I can't explain how I felt.

With the assistance of the Coast Guard, we anchored in the bay, secured everything, and changed our clothes. A shore boat came out to pick us up. We jumped in, and the pilot steered for the dock. As we got closer, we were blinded by a bunch of bright lights. There were a lot of people on the dock, and I spotted TV cameras—ABC, CBS, Channel 11, and more. When we reached the dock a group of reporters ran towards us and shoved microphones into our faces. The last thing I wanted to do was talk about what happened.

Fortunately, there were a few sailors that kept them at bay, and quickly escorted us to an office adjacent to a warehouse. They had coffee ready for us, and we all needed something to warm us up.

The first thing I wanted to do was call my parents to tell them I was OK. After seeing all the cameras and reporters, I was sure they knew about the incident.

Due to the storm, the phone lines were busy, and I had a lot of trouble getting through. Finally, I heard their phone ringing. My dad answered the phone.

"Hi, Dad"

Red Sky Morning

"Oh, thank God. Honey, it's Andy, he's alive! Are you OK?"

"Yeah, I'm fine, just tired. It's been a rough day."

I spoke to my mother, who was hysterical, but happy. Dad got back on the phone, and I told him the Coast Guard was going to take us back to their Port Hueneme headquarters by car. We would stay there for the night and be home the next day.

We arrived at the Coast Guard Station around three in the morning. They showed us to our bunks, and we all hit the sack.

I couldn't sleep. Every time I closed my eyes, I could see Bob floating below me, looking at me. I couldn't take it, so I got up and went into the living room. Frank and Nick were already up. We found some ice cream in the freezer and dished out some. We ate the ice cream and looked at each other, but no one said a word. Nick finally said he was going to try to sleep, while Frank and I stayed up a little longer, then headed for our bunks.

I guess I finally fell asleep, in fact, deeply. I awoke suddenly a sailor was shaking me. I asked him what he wanted. He said that he needed someone to go back to the *Diana*, because the anchor was dragging and it might hit the breakwater. He thought the rest of the crew was too whipped, but I was young and strong and should go. I leaped out of my bed and grabbed him by his jersey. The guy was a foot shorter then I was, and I lifted him off the ground, looked straight into his eyes, and said, "You know, I'm not really part of this crew. Let it sink."

The following morning, I found Anton sitting in the galley. I said good morning, and the captain responded with a grunt. He had bags under his red eyes and was staring off into the distance. These were not the eyes of a fisherman—searching, determined, excited and hopeful— but guilty, sad, dejected, and hopeless.

He looked up at me, and tears began to flow from his eyes. "I'm so sorry. You could have died, and it would have been my fault."

"We all could have drowned, but you did everything you could to save us, and Bob probably had a heart attack, because he didn't drown. You couldn't have saved him. Because of you and a few miracles, the rest of us survived."

"Oh Andy, thank you. Would you do me a favor?"

"Sure, what do you need?"

"Could you round up the guys. I want to go home."

In a half-hour we were on the road. Frank and I rode in the back, and Anton and Nick in the front. Frank was curled up on the bed of the truck and sleeping. I tried to sleep, but every time I closed my eyes, I still saw Bob, floating face up with that look of death. At that point, I knew I wouldn't be sleeping very well for the next few days.

Mom was in tears, and Dad was smiling when I walked in the door. We hugged, and they wanted to hear the whole story.

The next couple of days I sort of hid out, because everyone at school wanted to know what happened, and I wasn't in the mood to talk about it. On Wednesday morning, Duff called me.

"Hey, Andy, surf's up. You want to go to Royal Palms?

"Good idea. I'll meet you there."

I put on my trunks, threw my surf board on the racks of my Karmann Ghia. I loved that car, but I was determined to buy a Porsche before ski season started.

I drove down Paseo Del Mar and took the turnoff for Royal Palms. I drove down the hill and saw that the surf was definitely up; The conditions perfect. Duff was already there, waxing his board. I unhooked the straps grabbed my board. In five minutes, we were paddling out.

The waves were head high, and the one in front of me was starting to break. I paddled up the face, and the wave broke over me. As the wave passed, I continued to paddle. When I got past the break, I sat up and checked out the swells rolling in. That feeling of being alone crept into my mind, and chills started to run up and down my spine. The waves suddenly appeared giant and ugly, and it scared the hell out of me. I paddled to the shoulder of the next wave, rode it to shore on my belly, and got out of the water. I sat on a rock in disbelief, looking out at the waves, realizing what an impact the last weekend had on me.

When I got home, my mom told me that Bob's funeral was Friday at ten o'clock, and Mass was being held at Mary Star of the Sea Church. My parents didn't know the family that well and did not plan to attend, but recommended that I go.

I went by myself and sat with Frank. After the services, I paid my respects to Bob's wife and family. She got up and hugged me. We both cried while she thanked me for risking my life to save her husband.

The wake was held at the Yugoslav Hall. I had a few VO and Sevens, and by eight, I was ready to go home. I usually stayed up till ten or eleven, but the day had been mentally and physically draining, so I took a shower and went to bed.

As soon as my head hit the pillow, I went out like a light. I didn't know what time it was when I sat up in bed in a cold sweat. It was that recurring nightmare about Bob staring at me with his mouth and eyes wide open, trying to scream.

I was totally freaked out and prayed that it would go away. Little did I know that forty years later, there would be nights when that image would still return to haunt me.

Epilogue

I was surprised that everyone stayed awake. "Well, guys, that's the story, what'd you think?"

"Fantastic! You're damn lucky to be alive to tell it," said Bob.

Terry clapped. "You said it was a long story, but I loved every bit of it, and with our boat bouncing around and the wind whistling outside, I felt like I was right there."

Stretching and yawning, Joey said, "Yeah, and as you wrapped up the story our weather's starting to lie down and I'm about to do the same. See ya in the morning."

Everyone followed Joey to their bunks and got some rest. We woke up to a beautiful sunrise and calm waters, had a light breakfast, and started trolling. After an hour Bob yelled, "Hook up!" An hour and a-half later we had two hundred and twenty tuna on the deck. The skipper got on the P.A., "Reel' em in, it's time to head back home."

About the Author

Andrew J. Rafkin, was born in 1946 in San Pedro, California, and grew up in a commercial fishing family. Through high school, he worked on sport fishing boats, and at seventeen went commercial fishing with his father, captain of a large purse seiner, during summer vacation. Two years later, he worked aboard a ninety-foot fishing boat, which was caught in a hurricane force storm where Andrew almost lost his life.

These events later served as inspiration for his first nonfiction true life adventure, *Red Sky Morning*. Andrew served in the Navy during the Vietnam War and later graduated from California State University, Dominguez Hill with degrees in economics and marketing. He is a successful entrepreneur and President of a security company servicing Southern California over thirty years.

A voracious reader of Action-Adventure and Political Thrillers, Andrew decided to create his own story and characters and began to write Creating Madness, the first novel in the O.R.C.A. series. His second novel *Mediterranean Madness* will be available winter 2008.

Andrew and his wife live in San Pedro. Their home sits on the bluff overlooking the Pacific and Los Angeles and Long Beach harbors. Andrew spends his spare time reading, fishing, hunting, golfing, and making wine.

ALSO BY Andrew J. Rafkin

"Terrorists have attacked the harbor of Galveston, Texas, where a dirty bomb was detonated next to a container ship, resulting in major damage to the container ship, and the radiation released by the explosion could be disastrous. We have no further information at this time except that the president and the head of Homeland Security have pushed the terror alert to RED!

Andre Petrov, a successful security company executive, forms the Oceans Reconnaissance Commission and Associates (O.R.C.A.) to provide coastal and port protection against global terrorism, drug trafficking, and environmental issues.

Retired Navy SEAL Commander Reef Johansson and the beautiful Alexis Mikos, a former Greek Secret Service agent, plus a handpicked group of security and computer-specialists lead O.R.C.A. against the terrorists.

Using cutting-edge ballistics technology and specially designed and powerful Orca boats, they attempt to foil a diabolical terrorist plot funded and contrived by a vengeance-seeking North Korean family and a wealthy Iranian mullah.

**Learn more at: www.outskirtspress.com/
creatingmadness**

See original news headlines and
stories of that tragic day at sea!
www.andrewrafkin.com

Printed in the United States
126063LV00001B/2/P